CHRIST,
THE CROWN
OF THE
TORAH

CHRIST,
THE CROWN
OF THE
TORAH

Edward Earl Burgess

**Lamplighter
Books** from Zondervan
Publishing House
1415 Lake Drive, S.E., Grand Rapids, MI 49506

CHRIST, THE CROWN OF THE TORAH

This is a Lamplighter Book
Published by the Zondervan Publishing House
1415 Lake Drive, S.E., Grand Rapids, Michigan 49506

Library of Congress Cataloging in Publication Data

Burgess, Edward Earl.
  Christ, the crown of the Torah

  "A Lamplighter book"—T.p. verso
  Bibliography: p.
  1. Jesus Christ—Messiahship. I. Title.
BT230.B94 1986   232'.1   86-1726
ISBN 0-310-41621-3

Unless otherwise indicated, the Scripture text used is that of the King James Version, a version that still is characterized by beauty of cadence, readability, and reverence for God.

Edited by Wanda Dugan
Designed by Ann Cherryman

Printed in the United States of America

86 87 88 89 90 91 92 / 10 9 8 7 6 5 4 3 2 1

To my only earthly treasure,

my wife Jean
and our children,

Mark
Deborah
Janet
Joshua
Erin

whose lives, I pray, will always
be guided by the Word of God
and the Lord Jesus Christ,

and to

Rebecca Hatfield,

Bible teacher, personal friend,
saint of God, and former secretary,
whose tireless effort has made this book possible

CONTENTS

ACKNOWLEDGMENT

Special gratitude is extended to Marilyn Montgomery, a fantastic church secretary, who typed the special pages and corrected my errors.

PREFACE

Because I love the Bible and the Lord Jesus Christ, I love Israel and Jewish people. When I was young, I frequently visited Temple Beth Israel in San Diego, California, and since that time I have been drawn to the Jews. Further training at the Jewish Adult Institute of Temple Beth Emet in Anaheim, California enlarged my understanding of Hebrew customs and practices.

Today as Israel often dominates world news, one would expect the Christian church to learn more about the Jews. But Christian theologians have neglected to study the rabbis' writings in the Talmud. On the other hand, Jews have felt threatened by the name of Jesus as represented by Western Christendom. After all, the Holocaust took place in the birthplace of Protestant Christianity. What better reason for a modern Jew to run from Jesus?

This book seeks to narrow the gap between Jew and Christian. *Christ, The Crown of the Torah* draws a parallel between the royal Law of Israel (the Torah) and the royal subject of the Torah (Messiah Himself). Jesus of Nazareth will prove Himself to be that Messiah in two ways: by keeping every word of the Torah and by fulfilling its purpose as the living crown. The symbol is also borrowed from Judaism since it is believed that the study and practice of the Torah is the crown of any scholar.

Torah is the Hebrew word for "teaching." In the narrow sense it refers to the first five books of the Bible, otherwise called the Law of Moses or Pentateuch (five). Actually the Torah is not the law of Moses but the law of God. In a wider sense Torah can refer to all Jewish oral tradition and the writings of the rabbinic sages. This book generally uses Torah in the narrow sense or to refer to Old Testament writings.

"Gospel" is the English rendering of a Greek word meaning "good news." In the narrow sense, gospel refers to the birth, death, burial, and resurrection of Jesus. In a wider sense, the gospel is the totality of New Testament teaching, and it is with this meaning that this book uses the term.

I am not original; most subjects are documented elsewhere. But my intention has been to organize basic materials supporting the Messiahship of Jesus in a strict Hebrew framework. I am indebted to both Christian and Jewish sources.

My prayer is that both Christian and Jewish readers will be blessed. I pray especially that each reader will be drawn closer to the God of Israel and to the glory that is in Jesus the Messiah, the crown of the Torah.

Shalom,
Edward E. Burgess

Chapter 1

THE TORAH

Scripture for study:

Now these are the commandments, the statutes, and the judgments, which the LORD your God commanded to teach you, that ye might do them in the land whither ye go to possess it: That thou mightest fear the LORD thy God, to keep all his statutes and his commandments, which I command thee, thou and thy son, and thy son's son, all the days of thy life; and that thy days may be prolonged. Hear therefore, O Israel, and observe to do it; that it may be well with thee, and that ye may increase mightily, as the LORD God of thy fathers hath promised thee, in the land that floweth with milk and honey.

(Deut. 6:1–3)

Think not that I am come to destroy the law, or the prophets; I am not come to destroy, but to fulfill.

(Matt. 5:17)

Torah—the law of God. Amidst thunder, lightning, fire, smoke, earthquake, and trumpet blast, Moses received the law of God on Mount Sinai while the people of Israel trembled below (Deut. 6:1–3). For the first time, a nation received its constitution and laws directly from God. The Hebrews had been slaves under the Pharaohs of Egypt for 430 years. They had been free for only seven weeks. To a people who were "no people," God gave divine directions for a civilized social order and named them "a kingdom of priests, and a holy nation" (Exod. 19:6).

After receiving the original laws at Mount Sinai, Moses received additional revelation from God during the next forty years to complete the Torah. The final code of conduct taught men and women how to live in relationship to one another and to God. The laws directed moral, health, and civil codes; sacrificial and ceremonial guidelines; and details for celebrating religious festivals. The Torah promised blessings to the obedient, curses to the disobedient. God offered His love but demanded righteousness and justice in return. Israel agreed to God's terms—"all that the LORD hath spoken we will do" (Exod. 19:8) and entered into covenant with God.

While the Torah technically includes only the five books of Moses, or the Pentateuch, Torah often refers to the complete Hebrew Scriptures including the Prophets and the poetic writings. For the Jews, of course, the Old Testament is the only testament. It is the embodiment of Israel's faith.

DEVELOPMENT OF THE TALMUD

While Jews and Christians alike believe that Moses received the Written Torah at Sinai, Jewish tradition has long taught that he also received the Oral Torah. Moses then passed the Oral Torah, referred to as *Torah she-be-al peh*, first to Joshua, then to the elders of Israel, then to the prophets, and last to the men of the great assembly. The Oral Law supposedly refined and explained the general principles in the commandments. For example, the Written Torah said, "Thou shalt not take the name of the LORD thy God in vain" (Exod. 20:7). The Oral Torah described ways by which the divine name could be profaned. The Written Torah said, "Thou shalt not put a stumbling block in the path of the blind" (Lev. 19:14). The Oral Torah described ways by which one could injure or mistreat the blind.

Between A.D. 200 and 500 the Oral Torah was put into writing and became the Talmud. Both the Torah and the Talmud are authoritative in Jewish tradition.

REJOICING IN THE TORAH

Jews throughout history have rejoiced in the Torah and reverenced the Law. Today when the yearly cycle of study of the Torah is completed in the synagogue, the day becomes known as *Simhat Torah*, or "rejoicing in the Torah." Worshipers remove the scrolls of the Torah from the holy ark and parade around the synagogue seven times. They rejoice and sing. The children carry various types of banners, flags, and replicas of the Torah, and afterward they eat sweets to symbolize the sweetness of the Law of the Lord.

Jewish worshipers have also adorned the Torah for centuries with beautiful cloth coverings called mantels. They embroider the lions of Judah in silver or gold to depict the royal Law of the people of Israel. They roll the parchment scrolls of the Torah on wooden staves that are topped with ornate finials—silver crowns and bells. And finally the Jews include an elaborate breastplate and pointer. The breastplate, which hangs in front of the mantel by a silver chain, is often composed of engraved silver trees with strong roots. It symbolizes, "Her [Torah] ways are ways of pleasantness, and all her paths are peace. She is a tree of life to them that lay hold upon her: and happy is everyone that retaineth her" (Prov. 3:17–18). The *yad*, literally "hand," is the pointer, which hangs at the side of the plate. The *yad* is used to keep the parchment clean and to mark the place for the reader of the Torah.

Reading the Torah is the most important part of synagogue worship. The reading must be errorless and dignified. A section of the Law is read on the Sabbath, new moons and festivals, as well as every Monday and Thursday morning. The Torah is divided into fifty-four weekly sections to complete the reading in a year.

CHRIST INTERPRETS THE TORAH

In His Sermon on the Mount Jesus said, "Think not that I am come to destroy the law, or the prophets; I am not come to destroy, but to fulfill" (Matt. 5:17). He endorsed the Torah. He considered it the Word of God. His stated purpose to fulfill the Law was startling because no one had fulfilled it before Him. And Jesus indicated a letter-by-letter fulfillment. Not a "jot" (like an apostrophe) nor a "tittle" (the smallest part of a letter) would pass from the Law until the Law was accomplished. Jesus considered the Written Torah so sacred that not the smallest detail would go unfulfilled.

Oral tradition was in the formulative period when Jesus walked the earth. The Jews used the expression *the Law* to mean either the Ten Commandments, the five books of Moses, or to include the Law and the Prophets. But in confrontation with Jesus, the scribes also used it to mean the oral or scribal law.

Whereas the Torah gave broad principles like those found in the Ten Commandments, it expected the people to apply the principles to daily life. The scribes, who were the lawyers and recognized specialists of the Law, were not satisfied with the general moral guidance of the Torah. They reduced every great principle to thousands of rules and regulations. To serve God in the tradition of a strict Orthodox Jew or of a Pharisee meant keeping thousands of legalistic regulations never received by Moses or the Prophets, but created by the craft of the scribes. The Oral Law became so extensive that eventually it consisted of twelve printed volumes in the Jerusalem Talmud and sixty printed volumes in the Babylonian Talmud.

Jesus neither added to the Torah nor took away from it. He lived out its practical and intended meaning. For Him to "fulfill" it meant to "enforce" or to "express it in its full significance." Jesus adhered to the requirements of Moses, the Prophets, and the Writings, but He repeatedly broke scribal law. He censured the legalists because they could not fulfill their own requirements. For Jesus, petty rules and regulations like "It is not lawful to eat an egg laid on the Sabbath" could never satisfy the God of Israel. The Torah commanded animal sacrifice, but obedience to God was better than sacrifice. Showing love and mercy was better than being encumbered by a burdensome legal system.

Jesus fulfilled the Torah in two major ways. First, He kept all 613 commandments (as calculated by the rabbis). He was obedient to the moral, civil, health, ceremonial, and festival laws. Second, He fulfilled the prophetic word promising a Messiah. As He said of Himself, "These are the words which I spake unto you, while I was yet with you, that all things must be fulfilled, which were written in the law of Moses, and in the prophets, and in the psalms, concerning me" (Luke 24:44).

PAUL INTERPRETS THE TORAH

After Jesus' death and resurrection, the apostle Paul further developed the picture of the Messiah's fulfillment of the Torah. Once known as Rabbi Saul of Tarsus, esteemed member of the Pharisees, and most probably a young member of the Great Sanhedrin, Paul described his Jewish background: "Circumcised the eighth day, of the stock of Israel, of the tribe of Benjamin, an Hebrew of the Hebrews; as touching the law [Torah], a Pharisee; concerning zeal, persecuting the church; touching the righteousness which is in the law [Torah], blameless" (Phil. 3:5–6). Paul had received an excellent education in Tarsus and also in the Jerusalem rabbinical school under the great Rabban Gamaliel, grandson of Hillel. Paul was an expert not only in both the Torah and rabbinical arguments but also in the defense of the Torah.

After his conversion, Paul never repudiated the Torah, but he did declare a new interpretation. "For Christ is the end of the law [Torah] for righteousness to every one that believeth" (Rom. 10:4).

Paul admitted the Torah was holy, just, and good, but the Torah was unattainable because of the weakness of human nature. The fault rested not in God's Law but in human sin. What the Torah could not do for people, and what people could not do for themselves, God did by sending His Son. Jesus fulfilled the requirements of the Torah and brought redemption and justification to the believer. Paul taught that:

1. The Torah's function was to give a person a knowledge about his or her sin (Rom. 3:20).

2. The Torah is confirmed when it leads men and women to repentance and faith in Jesus (Rom. 3:31).

3. The Torah did not make Abraham right with God. He was justified by faith alone, 430 years before the Torah (Rom. 4:9–25).

4. The Torah exposes sin's power (Rom. 7:12–13).

5. The Torah was consummated in the Messiah. The righteousness that obedience to the Torah could not produce was supplied by faith in Jesus (Rom. 10:4).

6. The Torah was added (after Abraham's time) to put a check on sin (Gal. 3:19).

7. The Torah could not impart life or righteousness (Gal. 3:21).

8. The Torah was a tutor to teach men and women about their need for Jesus (Gal. 3:23–25).

9. The Torah consisted of elemental things to do until the Redeemer came to grant us adoption as His children (Gal. 4:3–5).

10. The Torah brought with it a yoke of bondage (inferred), but Jesus brought liberty (Gal. 5:1).

CROWN OF TORAH: CHRIST HIMSELF

In Old Testament times, the Jews lit their homes with lamps filled with burning olive oil, which produced a halo of fire called the *nezer* in Hebrew.

When a king was anointed with olive oil, it was as if his head was surrounded with a halo of fire, and the crown that he wore was a constant reminder of that bright halo. Thus the king became a symbol or a "lamp" to the nation.

A similar Hebrew word, *zer*, denoted the gold molding (or halo) that crowned the ark of the covenant. It was as if the Word of God in the ark—the Ten Commandments— was crowned. Thus the Commandments also became a "lamp" to the nation.

During later biblical times, the word *keter* became the popular expression for crown. The crown (*keter*) of the Torah conveyed two ideas. First, a person's study and practice of the Torah was the crowning spiritual exercise. Second, the Torah was a crown for Israel, a majestic lamp for the people of God.

To symbolize these ideas, rabbis decorated the Torah scrolls with an ornamental silver crown, which was circled by bells.

Christ became the living crown of the Torah. A descendant of Judah and David, He held a royal pedigree. The anointed Messiah King was surrounded by the *nezer,* and His life became a lamp to those who obeyed Him. He not only kept every commandment of the Torah, but He also completely fulfilled the Law. Christ adorned the Word of God in His practical living. He truly is the living Word, the crown of Israel, and the crown of the Torah.

Chapter 2

THE TORAH'S PROMISED SON

Scripture for study:

> *The scepter shall not depart from Judah, nor a lawgiver from between his feet, until Shiloh come; and unto him shall the gathering of the people be.*
>
> (Gen. 49:10)

> *Therefore the Lord himself shall give you a sign; Behold, a virgin shall conceive, and bear a son, and shall call his name Immanuel.*
>
> (Isa. 7:14)

> *But when the fulness of the time was come, God sent forth his Son, made of a woman, made under the law.*
>
> (Gal. 4:4)

The modern reader finds little or no excitement in a genealogy. Matthew, however, the gospel writer to the Jews, appealed to ancient Jewish mentality in Matthew

1:1. He started his account of the life of Jesus in the most natural way—with a family background, which was typical of Hebrew culture in that day.

The Jews were vitally interested in pedigrees. Jewish families possessed pedigrees that were guardedly accurate and that were needed to prove, for example, priestly descent. A Levitical priest was bound to prove an unbroken pedigree back to Aaron. When the priest married, his wife must produce a genealogy of at least five generations. Anyone whose genealogy included Gentile ancestry could lose his privileges as a Jew. Jewish genealogical records were guarded by the court of the Sanhedrin.

Both the Torah and the Prophets signaled that the Anointed One, or *Mashiah*, would emerge from the stock of Abraham, Jacob, Judah, and David. In Jewish literature *Mashiah* came to be the title for the king who would bring salvation and universal peace at the consummation of the age. When Matthew listed Abraham and David in the royal pedigree of Jesus, he sought the attention of the rabbis. He arranged the genealogy in three sections of fourteen generations each, for easy memorization. He also chose the divisions to point out three great epochs in the genealogical tree. The first was from Abraham to David; the second was from David to the Babylonian captivity; the third was from the Babylonian captivity to Messiah.

Writing specifically to the Jewish mind, Matthew listed a pedigree proclaiming Jesus the rightful heir and promised King of Israel, the crown of the Torah. The Jewish Talmud infers that Matthew gave Joseph's family background whereas Luke gave Mary's. Luke called Joseph the son of Heli. By marrying Mary, the daughter of Heli, Joseph became Heli's son (or his son-in-law).

JESUS, THE SON OF DAVID

Out of Jesus' extensive genealogy, one name carried the greatest importance to the Jews. Above all other requirements, they expected Mashiah to be a son of David. (Isa. 11:1). For that reason Matthew and the other authors of the New Testament referred to Jesus as the son of David. After Jesus healed the blind and dumb man, the Jews exclaimed, "Is not this the son of David?" (Matt. 12:23b). The Canaanite woman who pleaded for her daughter called Him, "son of David" (Matt. 15:22b). The blind men cried out, "Have mercy on us, O Lord, thou son of David" (Matt. 20:30, 31). The crowds greeted Him in Jerusalem as "son of David" (Matt. 21:9, 15). Peter stated this genealogical fact in his Pentecostal sermon (Acts 2:29–36). Paul said Jesus was a descendant of David (Rom. 1:3). John, when writing the Book of Revelation, heard Jesus say, "I am the root and the offspring of David" (Rev. 22:16b). Jesus was the credible son of David.

JESUS' NAME FULFILLED PROPHECY

Not only did Jesus' history fulfill messianic requirements, but His name also matched Jewish expectations. According to Jewish tradition a boy was named at the time of circumcision. The choice of a Hebrew name expressed to God the acknowledgment that the child was a gift from Him. It identified the child as a Jew and a member of Israel. The name expressed a desired hope for the destiny of the child.

Jesus was named by the angel Gabriel before His birth. His parents, in accord with tradition, confirmed the name at circumcision. The name Yeshua, or Joshua, meant

"Yahweh is salvation"; the name Jesus was the Greek equivalent.

The name Joshua was given to two other men mentioned in the Old Testament. Joshua, Moses' successor, led Israel to conquer Canaan (Josh. 11:23). Later another Joshua served as Israel's high priest after returning from bondage in Babylon (Hag. 1:1). Both were heroes. Both were associated with great deliverances.

Though the name Joshua, or Jesus, was a common Jewish name, Jesus alone lived up to its prophetic significance. The angel's message was, "for he shall save his people from their sins" (Matt. 1:21).

Today a full Hebrew name is given for religious and legal purposes and is to be specifically spelled out on Jewish documents. Since Jewish tradition uses the biblical style, the name of the son or daughter is always given with the name of the father. For example, a boy's name might be Samuel ben Gershom, meaning Samuel son of Gershom. Or a girl's name might be Leah bat Gershom, meaning Leah daughter of Gershom. If the father is from priestly or Levitical ancestry, the title "Ha-Kohen" or "Ha-Levi" is attached to the name. Examples are found in the names of two prominent rabbis who were descendants of the priestly tribe: Rabbi Shabbetai Ben Meir Ha-Kohen, a Lithuanian rabbi, who wrote a commentary on the code of Jewish law; and Rabbi David Ben Samuel Ha-Levi, who also wrote about Jewish law.

It is not acceptable for a Jew to take a Gentile or Christian name like Kris or Mary. Often a Jewish child is named in honor of a deceased loved one in order to perpetuate the relative's memory.

CIRCUMCISED ACCORDING TO THE LAW

In the Torah God commanded, "He that is eight days old shall be circumcised among you, every man child in your generations, he that is born in the house, or bought with money of any stranger, which is not of thy seed" (Gen. 17:12). Circumcision has been the sign of God's covenant with Israel since the time of Moses.

Today the ritual, called a *brit milah,* is still so important that it must be performed on the eighth day even if it falls on the Sabbath or on Yom Kippur, the Day of Atonement (exceptions are sickness of the child or weakness because of a premature birth). Jewish parents do not circumcise their sons merely for hygienic purposes. The father participates in the circumcision as a religious ceremony. A *mohel* (a Jew trained and certified for the procedure) performs the surgery either in a hospital or in the child's home. The mother is not present. Instead, a *minyan* (a quorum of ten Jews) observes the joyous occasion. One of these ten men (called a *sandek*) is given the honor of holding the child. If a *minyan* cannot be formed and the eighth day cannot be bypassed, the *brit* can be performed by the *mohel* in the father's presence only.

Any non-Jewish male who wished to convert to Judaism and who was already circumcised for hygienic purposes must undergo a symbolic or mock *brit.* This ceremony, called a *hatafat dam brit,* is performed by a *mohel* under the direction of the *bet din* (a rabbinical court of three persons). The *mohel* gives the male a pinprick to produce a spot of blood. Then the proper prayer is offered. Any Jewish child who was circumcised before or after the eighth day must also undergo a symbolic circumcision by a *mohel* in order for the circumcision to be legal. In this way the covenant of circumcision given to Abraham is confirmed.

Joseph obeyed the Torah and brought Jesus for circumcision when He was eight days old (Luke 2:21). Joseph initiated the first act that led to Jesus' fulfillment of the Torah.

REDEEMED ACCORDING TO THE LAW

The Torah said, "Sanctify unto me all the first-born, whatsoever openeth the womb among the children of Israel, both of man and of beast: it is mine" (Exod. 13:2). In keeping with this command, Jesus was offered to the Lord: "When the days of her purification according to the law of Moses were accomplished, they brought him to Jerusalem, to present him to the Lord; (As it is written in the law of the Lord, Every male that openeth the womb shall be called holy to the Lord;) And to offer a sacrifice according to that which is said in the law of the Lord, A pair of turtledoves, or two young pigeons" (Luke 2:22–24).

In the first giving of the Law, God required that all first-born sons of Israel were to be dedicated completely to His service. Remember that the first-born sons of Israel had escaped death during Egyptian bondage because their fathers had obeyed God's instructions and had sprinkled the blood of the lamb on the doorposts of their houses. First-born sons were especially precious to God. But God later took the priesthood out of the hands of the first-born males and designated the tribe of Levi as priests because of their faithfulness to Him in refusing to worship the golden calf (Num. 8:14–18). As a result, God allowed first-born sons to be bought back or "redeemed" from

God's ownership: "The first-born of man shalt thou surely redeem . . . and those that are to be redeemed from a month old shalt thou redeem, according to thine estimation, for the money of five shekels. . ." (Num. 18:15–16).

Today the ceremony, *Pidyon Haben* or "redemption of the son," still takes place. On the thirty-first day after his son's birth, the father either dedicates him to the service of the temple or redeems him. The redemption price is five shekels (five silver dollars), which he places next to the child in front of a *cohen*, the priest who must conduct the service. The *cohen* asks, "Which do you prefer, to give me your son or to redeem him?" The father answers, "To redeem him." The transaction is worked out and the son is redeemed. The redemption money is later used for charity.

"And when the days of her purification according to the law of Moses were accomplished, they brought him to Jerusalem, to present him to the Lord" (Luke 2:22). In keeping with the Law of her day, Mary waited out her purification period after childbirth, apparently thirty-three days after Jesus was circumcised (Lev. 12:1–5). During that time she did not enter the temple. Upon completion of the requirement, she brought the sacrifice—two young pigeons—as a token of her submission to the Torah.

Jesus was redeemed as the first-born son according to the Law. Since His family was of Judah and not Levi, He had to be redeemed. He could not serve the Lord as a temple priest. Yet His entire life was given to priestly service outside the temple. Mary and Joseph redeemed Him from Levitical service yet surrendered Him to God's work.

"And when they had performed all things according to the law of the Lord, they returned into Galilee, to their own city, Nazareth" (Luke 2:39). Mary and Joseph left nothing undone. They were obedient to the Torah, setting the pattern for Jesus.

COMING OF AGE ACCORDING TO THE LAW

Today a Jewish boy begins to take on adult responsibilities at the age of thirteen. At this point in his life he declares his faith in the Torah, shows his loyalty to his people, and chooses to be numbered among those of the household of Israel. He is *Bar Mitzvah*, a "son of the commandment."

At the ceremony in the synagogue, the *Bar Mitzvah* boy is called to the Torah. He considers it a great honor to be called to the Law of the Lord, and he reveals his desire to accept the responsibility of the religious life of a Jew. On the Sabbath of his *Bar Mitzvah*, he will read a portion of the Scriptures and chant a portion of the weekly lesson from the Prophets.

His father and his rabbi will have trained him in the wearing of the *tephillin*, the two small square leather boxes (containing passages from Exodus and Deuteronomy as a remembrance of the Law) worn on the forehead and left arm. The boy also will have learned to wrap himself in his *tallit* (prayer shawl) for morning prayer. If the boy is seriously dedicated to the religious life of a Jew, he will put on his *tephillin* and *tallit* every weekday morning for the ritual of prayer.

Bar Mitzvah, as known and practiced ceremonially today, was probably not known in Jesus' time. But whether recognized in ceremony or not, Jesus reached

His *Bar Mitzvah* time at twelve years old, on a visit to Jerusalem. "Now his parents went to Jerusalem every year at the feast of the passover. And when he was twelve years old, they went up to Jerusalem after the custom of the feast. . . . And it came to pass that, after three days, they found him in the temple, sitting in the midst of the doctors, both hearing them, and asking them questions. And all that heard him were astonished at his understanding and answers" (Luke 2:41–42, 46–47).

The Torah prescribed that all Jewish males must attend the three annual festivals—Passover (Unleavened Bread), Pentecost (Weeks), and Succoth (Tabernacles) (Exod. 23:14–17; Deut. 16:16). At Passover it was the custom of the Sanhedrin to meet for public discourse. The doctors of the Law would discuss and listen to all religious questions.

The scene of the young Messiah at the temple is one of "coming of age." Jesus reflected an unusual, intelligent grasp of the Torah. The rabbis had seen nothing like it before. His training from home and synagogue was mixed with divine intuition and inspiration. On the threshold of His manhood, Jesus recognized His unique relationship to God His Father. His messianic mission came into focus (Luke 2:49). The esteemed doctors of the Torah reckoned Him to be destined to an honorable position in the community of Israel. As Luke recorded it, "Jesus increased in wisdom and stature, and in favor with God and man" (Luke 2:52). He had become *Bar Mitzvah*, a Son of the Commandment.

Chapter 3

THE TORAH'S PROPHET

Scripture for study:

> *And the LORD said unto me . . . I will raise them up a*
> *Prophet from among their brethren, like unto thee,*
> *and will put my words in his mouth; and he shall*
> *speak unto them all that I shall command him. And it*
> *shall come to pass, that whosoever will not hearken*
> *unto my words which he shall speak in my name, I*
> *will require it of him.*
>
> (Deut. 18:17–19)

> *Then those men, when they had seen the miracle that*
> *Jesus did, said, This is of a truth that Prophet that*
> *should come into the world.*
>
> (John 6:14)

> *Many of the people, therefore, when they heard this*
> *saying, said, Of a truth this is the Prophet.*
>
> (John 7:40)

33

The old rabbis used to tell stories of hearing voices from heaven. They referred to this as *bat kol*, meaning "daughter [probably echo] of the voice [of God]." But when God spoke to Moses, He spoke face to face without mystic voices or echoes. For forty years Moses was a mighty prophet, acting not only as judge and shepherd to Israel but also as mediator between God and the people.

God revealed to Moses that another prophet would one day arise: "I will raise them up a Prophet from among their brethren, like unto thee, and will put my words in his mouth, and he shall speak unto them all that I shall command him" (Deut. 18:18). Although there were many prophets in Israel, none fulfilled all the ministries of Moses until Jesus. And Jesus exercised an original authority that went beyond even Moses.

The greatest Jewish teachers never claimed personal authority. The characteristic phrase of a scribe or rabbi was, "there is a teaching that . . ." or "according to rabbi . . ." or "the sages used to say. . . ." The scribes and rabbis never expressed an opinion unless it was supported by a quotation from the great sages of the past. Jesus, on the other hand, was His own authority. He claimed the right to point out religious error (Mark 7:6–13). His Sermon on the Mount was virtually a new Torah, not opposing the old, but expanding and applying it for the common person. Jesus spoke with a new authority: "And it came to pass, when Jesus had ended these sayings, the people were astonished at his doctrine; For he taught them as one having authority, and not as the scribes" (Matt. 7:28–29).

The Hebrew prophets who followed Moses, as great as they were, only reiterated the Torah. But like Moses, Jesus was lawgiver, mediator, judge, and shepherd.

Indeed, He was greater than Moses. People recognized Him to be "that Prophet" whom the Torah said would come (John 6:14; 7:40; Mark 8:28).

ELIJAH PREPARED THE WAY

While the Jews looked for a Messiah like the prophet Moses, they also expected the prophet Elijah to return to prepare the way. They pointed to Malachi 4:5–6 with a literal interpretation: "Behold, I will send you Elijah the prophet before the coming of the great and dreadful day of the LORD; And he shall turn the heart of the fathers to the children, and the heart of the children to their fathers, lest I come and smite the earth with a curse."

Jews at the time of Christ expected Elijah to pave the way for peace during the messianic age. Jewish tradition said he would bring manna from the wilderness, a jug of oil and water that had been used to anoint the Tabernacle, and the budding rod of Aaron, which had been kept in the ark of the covenant. Manna would be used for food during the messianic age; oil would anoint the Messiah; and Aaron's rod would serve as His scepter.

But according to the New Testament, the way-maker of the Messiah appeared in John the Baptist. John came in the style, demeanor, spirit, power, preaching form, and image of the prophet Elijah. He was also a *cohen*, a priest. His Hebrew name was Johanan, the son of (ben) Zechariah. His father was of the family of Abijah (1 Chron. 24:10, Luke 1:5), most probably a descendant of Eleazer and, in turn, a descendant of Aaron. Thus, in John the Baptist was a combination of priest and prophet, just like Elijah. As Luke recorded it, "And thou, child, shalt be called the prophet of the Highest: for thou shalt go before the face of the Lord to prepare his ways; To give knowledge of salvation unto his people by the remission of their sins . . ." (Luke 1:76–77). Jesus Himself declared John to be Elijah. "For all the prophets and the law prophesied until John. And if ye will receive it, this is Elias, which was for to come" (Matt. 11:13–14).

JOHN'S BAPTISM

The rabbis who anticipated Elijah expected him to bring a message of repentance and charity. They looked to him to settle legal disputes and put an end to sin. In fact, some rabbis said that if Elijah led Israel to repentance for one day, Messiah would come.

John the Baptist did bring a message of repentance and charity. He did declare God's judgment. But his emphasis on personal repentance and baptism was not what the Jews expected.

Baptism or ceremonial cleansing began with God's instruction to the priests in the tabernacle. He commanded them to bathe before entering the Holy Place, when commissioned as priests, and on the Day of Atonement (Yom Kippur). Through ceremonial cleansing, the priesthood demonstrated to Israel that men and women were by nature unclean. Before coming to the Lord, even priests had to be symbolically purified. The cleansing did not remove their sins in any literal sense, but it was an object lesson of the constant need for cleansing. Sanctification is necessary before men and women can approach God. The hands and feet, as well as the heart, of those who minister to God and others must be clean.

During the intertestamental period a Jewish sect (probably Essenes) practiced ritual baths at Qumran, as revealed in the archeological discovery of the Dead Sea Scrolls. The large open baptistries found among their ruins indicate the prominent place of full immersion cleansing in this sect, which was still functioning in John the Baptist's time.

Today Jewish baptism continues. According to tradition a *mikveh* (place of purification) is considered more important in a Jewish community than a synagogue. Women must bathe for purification at prescribed times; proselytes are also baptized. On the afternoon of Rosh Hashana (New Year's Day), dedicated Jews perform a symbolic 'baptism' by shaking their garments into water as a sign of repentance and casting off sin.

But John's baptism was neither proselyte baptism to Judaism nor a ritual of purification. God gave John a ministry of preaching repentance and a "new" baptism as an act of that repentance. John received a divine directive according to Luke 3:2: "And the word of God came unto John the son of Zechariah in the wilderness." John's baptism was a mark of regeneration of the heart.

Since John was the last prophet under the old covenant, Jesus submitted to his baptism. But if Jesus needed no repentance, why was He baptized? First, He identified with those being baptized, with men and women and their condition. Second, He marked His ordination to public ministry with the baptism. John anointed Him as Messiah. Third, His baptism was an act of obedience to John's heavenly commission. Jesus did not need regeneration, repentance, or cleansing. But through baptism John (as Elijah) sanctioned Jesus as Messiah—the prophet like Moses—for whom the Jews were waiting.

A PROPHET IN THE SYNAGOGUE

After His baptism, Jesus next declared Himself as the great Prophet in a most logical place—His own synagogue. The synagogue, or *Beth Knesset* (a "house of assembly"), emerged during the Babylonian exile in the sixth century before Christ. After the temple of Solomon had been destroyed, the Jews were without a central place of worship, so they gathered in small assemblies to keep the faith of Israel alive. By the time of Christ, Jewish sages considered each local synagogue as a "little sanctuary," second only to the temple.

Daniel 6:10 tells us that while he was in captivity, Daniel prayed toward Jerusalem because the central sanctuary had been there. The Holy of Holies, then in ruins, had been the heart of the geographical territory of Judaism. As a result of this, the Jewish Talmud instructs that if a person is outside of Israel, that person is to pray facing Jerusalem, the site of the temple. Synagogues outside of Israel are planned so the holy ark, containing the Torah, is on the eastern wall of the sanctuary.

The original ark of the covenant contained not only the tablets of stone upon which were engraved the Ten Commandments but also most probably the Book of the Covenant given to Moses. The ark was the most precious and important article of furniture in the tabernacle (and later the temple) and was placed in the Holy of Holies, separated from the rest of the tabernacle by a heavy veil. The ark was a gold-plated chest whose lid, called the mercy seat, was covered by two gold cherubim.

Fashioned after the tabernacle, the synagogue was built around a veiled ornate chest called the "holy ark," which contained the scrolls of the Torah. A raised platform, or *bimah,* located in the front-center of the synagogue provided a focus for reading and preaching from the Torah. In front of the holy ark an "eternal light," or *Ner Tamid,* burned continually, symbolizing the spiritual enlightenment that emanates from the Torah. A candelabrum reminiscent of the seven-branched lampstand, or *menorah,* was also lighted.

Modern synagogue personnel include the rabbi, the cantor, the sexton, and the *gabbai* (the synagogue president). The rabbi is trained in the Torah, the Talmud, and codes of Jewish law and is thereby the head of the Jewish community. The cantor leads the congregation in prayer, supervises the choral program, and when no educational director is available, the cantor also leads the synagogue school. The sexton helps to supervise the daily services. He attends to the scrolls, Bibles, prayer books, shawls, and *kippahs* (skull caps) for visitors. He frequently serves as the Torah reader and must therefore be proficient in reading Hebrew. The *gabbai,* the president of the board of directors, manages the financial matters of the congregation.

Through the years the synagogue has been a house of assembly, a house of prayer, and a house of study. It also served as a court of justice and had the power to scourge lawbreakers. The synagogue later developed into a center of welfare and community affairs—the heart of Jewish social life.

During Jesus' time, worship in the Nazareth synagogue probably consisted of reciting the *Shema,* which was the creed of Israel (Deut. 6:4–9). The *Shema* was followed by a fixed prayer, a fixed selection from the Torah, a free selection from the Prophets, as well as an exposition and application of both Scripture portions. The service would conclude with a priestly blessing given by a *cohen*. The Scripture was first read in the sacred Hebrew language and then was translated into the local language, Aramaic. Since the synagogues had no official rabbis in those days, the ruler of the synagogue or the elders customarily invited any competent Jew to stand and read the Scriptures, then to sit down and explain. (Since Jesus both read the Scripture and preached, He must have spoken both Hebrew and Aramaic.)

Jesus had been a member of the Nazareth synagogue most of His life. Since He had trained in the Torah there, He was no stranger to the officials or other members of the synagogue. According to Luke 4:16, His parents had taught Him to worship there: "As his custom was, he went into the synagogue on the sabbath day."

On this occasion recorded by Luke, Jesus declared that He was the fulfillment of Isaiah's prophecy (Isa. 61:1–2): "The Spirit of the Lord is upon me, because he hath anointed me to preach the gospel to the poor; he hath sent me to heal the broken-hearted, to preach deliverance to the captives, and recovering of sight to the blind, to set at liberty them that are bruised, to preach the acceptable year of the Lord. . . . And he began to say unto them, This day is this scripture fulfilled in your ears" (Luke 4:18–19, 21).

He was the Prophet foretold by the Torah—the Prophet who would succeed Moses. He was also the Prophet foretold by Isaiah. This self-disclosure opened His public teaching ministry. The structure of the synagogue services provided a natural preaching station for Jesus. He taught the gospel of the kingdom and healed the sick. But the synagogues also opposed Him and questioned His authority.

When Jesus announced that He was the fulfillment of messianic prophecy, the members of His synagogue were furious. According to Luke 4:29 they "rose up, and thrust him out of the city." Although an official excommunication was not described, Jesus was apparently put out of the synagogue. Those of the community who claimed He was the promised Messiah were also excommunicated from the synagogue (John 9:22, 34). Another of Isaiah's prophecies was fulfilled in Him: "He is despised and rejected of men" (Isa. 53:3).

Rejection from the synagogue was most humiliating during the rabbinic period between 300 B.C. and A.D. 500. While there were several degrees of banishment, the most severe was *herem* (anathema), or excommunication from society, for an indefinite period. The person under anathema had to act as if he or she were in mourning. The excommunicated person could not wash or eat with the family. If the offender did not repent after three warnings, charges were drawn up and read in the synagogue. Candles were lit and the ram's horn was blown. The candles were then put out and the notice of excommunication was posted. On occasion the violator of Jewish law was scourged. Jesus warned His disciples to expect scourging in the synagogues (Matt. 10:17).

Jesus experienced *herem* when the synagogue in which He grew up banished Him from their midst. The temperament of the officials was so ruthless, they could have taken His life (Luke 4:28–29). The biblical record gives no reference to an official ban, but in practice His excommunication was official.

Today the most severe form of excommunication from family life is sitting *shivah*. This form of excommunication takes place when a family member has violated Jewish values without repentance and is thus considered dead. The mourning for the excommunicated person is expressed in sitting *shivah*, sitting on low stools for seven days. In extreme cases a family will practice *shivah* when a Jew marries a Gentile or when a Jew leaves the Jewish faith.

Jesus was a rabbi, a miracle-working prophet, the Son of God. The greatness of His teaching, His insight into the truth, and His knowledge of the human heart compelled many people to address Him as "Rabbi." The meaning of the title is more than just a teacher. It more properly means "my great one" or "my master." John the Baptist's disciples said to Christ, "Rabbi, . . . where dwellest thou?" (John 1:38). Christ's own disciples said, "Rabbi, when camest thou hither?" (John 6:25). Nicodemus, a cautious and learned member of the Supreme Court, expressed his personal judgment of Christ when he said, "Rabbi, we know that thou art a teacher come from God" (John 3:2). When Nicodemus addressed Jesus with this honorific title, he spoke his approval of this teacher who had never attended the traditional rabbinic schools of the day. Jesus' miracles and public teaching placed Him above the scholars and sages of the time. He was a rabbi of first rank, without equal.

After the destruction of the temple in Jerusalem, the sages who were interpreters of the Torah came to be known as the *tannaim*. Those who became specialists were given the title of "Rabbi" or were called "doctors of the law." Before the time of Jesus, Rabbi Shammai and Rabbi Hillel were two noted sages. Shammai and his followers were conservative in their interpretation of the Torah while Hillel and his followers held more liberal views.

Jesus, a master rabbi, was an expert in the Torah.

Jewish tradition says that the Torah confers authority on the spiritual leader in the community and places him in the position of judge. Since a rabbi is trained in the law, he is expected to judge in spiritual questions. Jesus, therefore, was a qualified, gifted, and natural judge over the religious affairs of men and women.

Chapter 4

THE TORAH'S POWERFUL SERVANT

Scripture for study:

> *And it shall come to pass, if they will not believe thee,*
> *neither hearken to the voice of the first sign, that they*
> *will believe the voice of the latter sign. And it shall*
> *come to pass, if they will not believe also these two*
> *signs, neither hearken unto thy voice, that thou shalt*
> *take of the water of the river, and pour it upon the dry*
> *land; and the water which thou takest out of the river*
> *shall become blood upon the dry land. . . . Thus saith*
> *the* LORD, *In this thou shalt know that I am the* LORD:
> *behold, I will smite with the rod that is in mine hand*
> *upon the waters which are in the river, and they shall*
> *be turned to blood.*
>
> (Exod. 4:8–9; 7:17)

> *Jesus saith unto them, Fill the waterpots with water.*
> *And they filled them up to the brim. And he saith*
> *unto them, Draw out now, and bear unto the*

governor of the feast. And they bore it. When the ruler of the feast had tasted the water that was made wine, and knew not whence it was (but the servants which drew the water knew,) the governor of the feast called the bridegroom, and saith unto him, Every man at the beginning doth set forth good wine, and when men have well drunk, then that which is worse; but thou hast kept the good wine until now. This beginning of miracles did Jesus in Cana, of Galilee, and manifested forth his glory; and his disciples believed on him.

(John 2:7–11)

Jesus' first miracle was very much like Moses' first miracle against Egypt. Whereas Moses turned water to blood, Jesus turned water to wine. Whereas Moses proclaimed judgment and wrath, Jesus brought blessing and grace. Whereas Moses demonstrated terror of the Lord, Jesus offered His joy. In each way Jesus, the "prophet like unto Moses," surpassed the power of Moses' miracle.

MESSIAH'S FIRST SIGN

Jesus performed His first miracle at the wedding of an unnamed couple in an unimposing village—Cana of Galilee. The marriage probably began on a Wednesday, according to custom, and it may have continued for seven days. Also according to custom, the family of the wedding party served wine. The rabbis used to say, "Without wine there is no joy." Although drunkenness was denounced by all the prophets, wine was essential to the religious celebrations of life. In the time of Christ, most

Jews drank fermented grape juice—two parts wine to three parts water. A host offered wine to his guests as a sacred duty of hospitality on nearly every occasion. At a wedding feast, the bride and groom would be publicly embarrassed if the wine supply ran out.

Jesus and His disciples probably arrived at the end of the wedding celebration in Cana; His mother told Him of the need for wine. "And there were set there six waterpots of stone, after the manner of the purifying of the Jews, containing two or three firkins apiece" (John 2:6). Josephus, the Jewish historian, says that a *firkin* was equivalent to about nine gallons. The large stone jars contained about twenty gallons each or one hundred twenty gallons in total. Strict Jews used these jars for ceremonial cleansing. Jesus ordered the ritual jars to be filled to the top; then He asked the servants to "draw out" a sample. When the head waiter tasted the water made wine, he marveled at the excellent quality of the vintage. "Every man at the beginning doth set forth good wine and, when men have well drunk, then that which is worse; but thou hast kept the good wine until now" (John 2:10).

Messiah introduced His presence with the ancient symbol of joy—the best wine—while supplying a practical human need. The rabbis believed that the "days of Messiah" would be like the joy of a wedding feast. Jesus fulfilled that expectation; He sanctified marriage and shared earthly joy with His first sign as Israel's Messiah. His attendance at the wedding revealed something of the social life that characterized His ministry. Jesus said John the Baptist "came neither eating nor drinking" while He Himself "came eating and drinking" (Matt. 11:18, 19). Unlike John, Jesus readily chose a nonascetic lifestyle.

Christ entered into the happy moments of life without inhibitions. He sometimes banqueted with friends, and without guilt He ate with known sinners. Ultimately Messiah Himself would furnish the feast and invite His friends to come and share it with Him (Luke 14:16–24).

Jewish Marriage Customs

The Hebrew word for marriage is *kiddushin*, meaning sanctification or holiness. Marriage is considered a sacred union between two equal persons, each of whom is involved in the planning of the wedding.

The Niddah

Under the Mosaic law, the wedding is carefully planned to avoid the time of separation during the menstrual period (Lev. 18:19). The Torah prohibits intimate relations during this period of separation. The Talmud teaches that the time is extended to a period of "seven clean days" after the menstrual period.

The Fasting

An ancient Hebrew custom requires the bride and groom to fast on their wedding day until after the ceremony, signifying the self-purification and spiritual preparation before starting married life together. Weddings cannot be planned for the Sabbath, religious festivals, or regular fast days.

The Dowry

Hebrew tradition dictates that the wife furnishes the new home with a closet, table, and bed as her part of the agreement. The groom, on the other hand, provides her with protection, care, and freedom from want.

In some countries the betrothed couple exchange gifts before the wedding. The groom gives his bride a prayer book, fine haircombs, and a veil. The bride gives her groom a prayer shawl and a Passover service book (a *Haggadah*).

The betrothal period usually lasts from a month to a year. This engagement time allows the parents of both the bride and the groom to arrange the conditions of the marriage. The dowry and penalties for breaking the agreement are fixed during this time. A matchmaker (a *shadchan*) functions as the marriage broker who guarantees that all parties are satisfied. His fee is a small percentage of the dowry.

The Huppah

The Jewish wedding ceremony is performed under a canopy called a *huppah*, symbolizing the unity of the husband and wife under the same roof in their new home. Canopies can be made of flowers or most appropriately, a large prayer shawl held up by four poles or four attendants.

The Head Covering

The Jewish wedding custom requires all men to wear hats or caps. *Kippahs* (skull caps) are provided for the men if the ceremony is held in the synagogue. The bride normally wears a veil.

The Ketubah

The Jewish marriage contract, called a *ketubah*, is drawn up before the wedding and is read as part of the ceremony. This legal document, which spells out the husband's obligations to support and care for his wife, is binding until divorce or death.

The Ring

The traditional wedding ring is a simple ring without diamonds or other jewels. Some rings may include Hebrew inscriptions about love. The ring may not be borrowed and must be fully paid for before the groom gives it to the bride.

Giving the Bride Away: No!

The bride is not "given away" according to Jewish custom. Instead, her parents merely accompany her to the *huppah*.

The Service

The simple ceremony under the *huppah* follows this general pattern:

1. The welcoming benediction prayers to the bride and groom are recited.

2. The blessing is offered over the first glass of wine.

3. The groom places the ring on the bride's finger and says, "Be sanctified to me with this ring in accordance with the laws of Moses and Israel."

4. The marriage agreement (*ketubah*) is read.

5. The Seven Benedictions are recited, which must be done in the presence of a *minyan* (quorum of ten Jews).

6. The groom breaks the glass (a sign lamenting the fact that the temple in Jerusalem is destroyed and still in ruins).

When the guests leave the wedding scene, they speak best wishes to the couple by saying, "May your constellations be favorable to you." It is important to make the couple merry and happy. At the reception, as practiced by the Hasidim, the men dance with the men and the women dance with the women.

MESSIAH'S GREATEST SIGN

Jesus the Messiah performed greater signs than Moses. Moses never raised the dead; rather he pronounced death to the unprotected first-born children in Egypt. Jesus the Messiah also performed greater works than the prophets. The prophet Elijah breathed life back into the body of the widow's son (1 Kings 17:19–22). Elisha revived the Shunammite woman's son (2 Kings 4:32–35). But the Scriptures teach that Jesus raised the dead three times: the son of the widow of Nain (Luke 7:11–15); Lazarus, the brother of Mary and Martha (John 11:41–44); and the twelve-year-old daughter of Jairus (Mark 5:37–43). Jesus' power to raise the dead attested to His claim as Messiah.

In the case of Jairus's daughter, Jesus responded to a synagogue official. Jairus was likely the president, or *gabbai*, whose responsibility it was to care for the physical properties of the synagogue. He stripped himself of pride, took courage against public opinion, and as a last resort sought the aid of Jesus, a prophet unrecognized by the synagogue. "And, behold, there cometh one of the rulers of the synagogue, Jairus by name; and when he saw him, he fell at his feet, and besought him greatly, saying, 'My little daughter lieth at the point of death. I pray thee, come and lay thy hands on her, that she may be healed; and she shall live'" (Mark 5:22–23).

The little girl was twelve years old. According to Jewish tradition, a girl takes on responsibility to the Torah at twelve—she reaches adulthood. On the threshold of womanhood, Jairus's daughter died before Jesus could reach her. The professional mourners had been summoned because the obligation to lament the dead was a high priority among the Jews. The mourners tore their clothes; they wailed. Minstrels or flutists added to the sad lament. The Talmud said, ". . . the very poorest amongst the Israelites will not allow her [the dead party] less than two flutists and one wailing woman; but if he be rich, let all things be done according to his qualities." Thus, the house of the synagogue official was in mourning.

Jesus responded to Jairus and followed him to his house.

> *And when he was come in, he saith unto them, Why make ye this ado, and weep? the damsel is not dead, but sleepeth. And they laughed him to scorn. But when he had put them all out, he taketh the father and the mother of the damsel, and them that were with him, and entereth in where the damsel was lying. And he took the damsel by the hand, and said unto her, Talitha cumi; which is, being interpreted, Damsel, I say unto thee, arise.*
>
> (Mark 5:39–41).

Jesus said she was asleep. That was a common Jewish euphemism for death, but the wailing crowd took Jesus literally and laughed at His supposed naïveté. They mourned the dead while laughing to scorn the Messiah.

Although priests would not touch the dead out of fear of defilement (Lev. 21:1–4), Jesus took the hand of the dead girl and brought her to life. He who formed the body of Adam out of clay and breathed life into him could touch death and bestow life. Jesus demonstrated His power as Messiah and verified a coming resurrection day for all the people of God.

God had said to Moses, "If they will not believe thee, neither hearken to the voice of the first sign, . . . they will believe the voice of the latter sign" (Exod. 4:8). Messiah's first sign was changing water into wine. Messiah's greatest sign was raising the dead. Yet Israel, like Egypt, did not believe. Only a few of a "mixed multitude" escaped God's wrath and left Egypt with Moses and Israel. Likewise, only a few in Capernaum believed the signs of the Torah's powerful servant and received Him as the promised Messiah (Matt. 11:23–24).

Jewish Funeral Customs

When death occurs, the rabbi or cantor, rather than the mortician, is called first. The eyes of the deceased are closed, and the body is taken from the bed and placed on the floor. The body is never left alone until burial.

The family contacts a Jewish funeral home for the customary kosher burial. Jewish belief dictates that great care and honor be given to the dead body because it was the abode of the spirit. Autopsies are forbidden because they desecrate the body. If an autopsy is ordered for legal reasons, it can be done only with the consent of the family of the deceased.

The burial society carefully washes the body (see references to Dorcas in Acts 9:37) and anoints the forehead with egg yolks, the symbol of immortality. The body is wrapped in a simple white shroud, indicating that distinctions between rich and poor are erased in death. The men are also wrapped in their prayer shawls (*tallit*). But death ends all obligations to the Torah. The fringes on the shawl, representing the commandments of the Lord, are thus buried with the observant Jew. Embalming is forbidden under Jewish law. The whole body, including the blood, must be buried. Cremation is not an option because it also is forbidden by the Torah.

Burial

Expensive burials are discouraged; dignity with simplicity is the rule. The Orthodox Jew is buried in a simple wooden casket held together with glue or wooden pegs instead of nails. The casket remains closed because the Jewish sages considered it a dishonor for anyone to look into the face of a dead person. A light is kindled and set at the head of the casket to symbolize the immortality of the soul.

Burial takes place as soon as possible, not later than twenty-four hours after death. No burials, however, are allowed on the Sabbath or on the first days of any of the religious festivals.

The Cohen

Jewish law prescribes that Jewish priests are forbidden to come into contact with a dead body (Lev. 21:1–4). The priests are not even allowed to come into the same room with a dead body. Even at the cemetery, the Jewish priest cannot come within six feet of the grave. Special allowance is made for the priest if the dead person is a close relative.

Mourning

Sitting *shivah* is the Jewish custom of sitting on low stools or cushions for seven days as a sign of lamenting the loss of a loved one. Jews also express grief by tearing a garment or by wearing a piece of black ribbon on the lapel.

Jewish customs prescribe three periods of mourning: the first seven days, the first thirty days, and the last eleven months. For the first seven days after the funeral, the mourners stay at home and sit on low stools. They wear no shoes made of leather, take no baths, and have no sexual intercourse during this time. For seven days all mirrors are covered because they reflected the image of the dead person. To remind them of future hope, the mourners eat hard-boiled eggs (the symbol of life) and keep a candle continuously lit. The mourners do not study the Torah for the seven-day period, but they do attend the Sabbath service.

During the first thirty days after the funeral, the mourners engage in no entertainment. They attend no parties, play no music, and are involved in no weddings. They do not shave or cut their hair for the thirty-day period.

The last period of mourning stops on the anniversary of the death. The sons recite the *Kaddish* memorial prayer in a daily service in the presence of a *minyan*. The prayer is said not as a prayer for the dead but as a memorial in honor of deceased parents.

We have no record that Messiah ever practiced sitting *shivah*. Assuredly Jesus was touched by the sorrow of death. When His friend Lazarus died, Jesus wept (John 11:35). He cried because of the nature of death; He had temporarily lost a friend. He also cried because of the deep grief that Mary and Martha experienced when their brother Lazarus died. But Jesus was not afraid of death. Instead, the life-giver readily touched the dead body of Jairus's daughter, and in this gesture He expressed His power over death.

Chapter 5

THE TORAH'S HOLY OBSERVANT

Scripture for study:

Now therefore hearken, O Israel, unto the statutes and unto the judgments, which I teach you, for to do them, that ye may live, and go in and possess the land which the LORD God of your fathers giveth you. Ye shall not add unto the word which I command you, neither shall ye diminish aught from it, that ye may keep the commandments of the LORD your God which I command you.

(Deut. 4:1–2)

Behold my servant, whom I uphold; mine elect, in whom my soul delighteth; I have put my spirit upon him; he shall bring forth judgment to the Gentiles. He shall not cry, nor lift up, nor cause his voice to be heard in the street. A bruised reed shall he not break, and the smoking flax shall he not quench; he shall bring forth judgment unto truth. He shall not fail nor

*be discouraged, till he have set judgment in the earth;
and the isles shall wait for his law.*

(Isa. 42:1–4)

*Think not that I am come to destroy the law, or the
prophets; I am not come to destroy, but to fulfill. For
verily I say unto you, Till heaven and earth pass, one
jot or one tittle shall in no wise pass from the law, till
all be fulfilled"* (Matt. 5:17–18).

To the observant Jew, the Torah is more than the five
books of Moses; it is a body of law, the constitution of
Israel, and the foundation of Jewish tradition. The term
Torah refers not only to the entire tradition and the entire
Bible (Old Testament) but also to the postbiblical traditions, which are still being written. Actually the term
Torah means "teaching," the whole body of revelation
and tradition. Jews rarely refer to the Bible; instead they
refer to the Torah, the whole body of both biblical and
rabbinic teaching.

Jesus, the "prophet like unto Moses," who fulfilled the
prophecy of the Torah and validated His claims as
Messiah with mighty miracles, also kept the Law perfectly
and completely. Jesus, the Torah's holy observant, kept
the biblical Torah. He rejected the traditions and additions created by the elders, scribes, and rabbis, but He
observed and loved the Mosaic law with unflinching
loyalty.

THE LAW OF SABBATH

The Torah stated, "Remember the sabbath day, to keep
it holy. Six days shalt thou labor and do all thy work; but

the seventh day is the sabbath of the LORD thy God: in it thou shalt not do any work, thou, nor thy son, nor thy daughter, nor thy manservant, nor thy maidservant, nor thy cattle, nor thy stranger that is within thy gates" (Exod. 20:8–10). Instruction from the Torah was simple. For the Sabbath to be different (holy) from other days, neither person nor beast was to work on that day. Several prophets commented further on the Sabbath. Both Jeremiah (Jer. 17:21) and Nehemiah (Neh. 13:19) condemned trading on the Sabbath, especially as it involved carrying burdens. Jewish sages later drew up thirty-nine different classifications of work. One classification that involved carrying a burden argued that carrying such items as a needle, a brooch, or even an artificial leg or tooth was in violation of the Torah.

The sages wished to protect the Sabbath from careless violations. They affectionately called the day a "queen" or "bride." Rabbinic law forbade, among the thirty-nine restrictions: cooking, baking, carrying, moving, pushing, grinding, chopping, straining, digging, planting, weeding, washing, drying, fishing, netting, trapping, knitting, sewing, constructing, repairing, writing, drawing, painting, cutting, tearing, haircutting, shaving, kindling, and burning.

Today the list of restrictions includes reading business material, participating in athletic activities, watching TV, buying and selling, riding an animal, sailing, playing an instrument, turning lights on and off, handling money, traveling, and planning post-Sabbath activity.

In Jesus' day neither the Torah nor the Jewish interpretation of it forbade righteous works on the Sabbath. Even the Talmud saw the need for healing on the day of rest: "The Torah gave permission to the physician to heal;

moreover, this is a religious precept and it is involved in the category of saving life."*

But carrying things on the Sabbath was another matter. Jesus encountered a difficulty with this law of oral tradition:

> And a certain man was there, which had an infirmity thirty and eight years. When Jesus saw him lie, and knew that he had been now a long time in that case, he saith unto him, Wilt thou be made whole? The impotent man answered him, Sir, I have no man, when the water is troubled, to put me into the pool; but while I am coming, another steppeth down before me. Jesus saith unto him, Rise, take up thy bed, and walk. And immediately the man was made whole, and took up his bed, and walked; and on the same day was the sabbath. The Jews, therefore, said unto him that was cured, It is the sabbath day; it is not lawful for thee to carry thy bed.
>
> (John 5:5–10)

Compelled by mercy, the great physician brought health and life to the man on the Sabbath. Jesus pursued the spirit of the Sabbath, kept Jewish law, healed the lame man, and glorified God. But the Jewish Mishnah, containing the thirty-nine prohibitions against work on the Sabbath, was broken. It allowed carrying a man on a pallet, but the pallet itself could not be carried. The rabbis taught that the Sabbath law could be relaxed if it meant the health and saving of life. But they had made the

*Berakhot 60a; Shulhan Arukh, Yoreh Deah 336:1.

interpretation of Jeremiah 17:21 and Nehemiah 13:19 so intricate and sophisticated that an unlearned layperson would surely fail. Jesus' critics accepted His works of mercy but condemned His command to carry the pallet home. Again, did the Torah allow for exceptions for acts of mercy or necessity? It can be reasoned from the law that God rested from His creative acts on the seventh day, but His higher works of mercy, sustenance, judgment, and compassion went on even on the Sabbath. Philo, who wrote in the first Christian century, observed, "God never leaves off making, but even as it is the property of fire to burn and snow to chill, so it is the property of God to make"—even on the Sabbath. Philo also said, "God never ceases to create nor takes a holiday from His works." The solar system functions every day. Rivers flow to the ocean. God causes it to rain and shine. He gives power to the flowers to germinate and grow. He causes the slow process of healing in the body to take place. Babies are born—what labor! All on the Sabbath. The holy day reflects the glorious activity of a caring God.

Jesus encountered Jewish leaders on the subject of the Sabbath many times. Certainly He kept the carpenter shop closed on the Sabbath. He gave Himself to the worship services in the synagogue. But Jesus also identified with the Creator by continuously showing special grace, by conferring health, happiness, and life to the people He met. His mission as Israel's Messiah-Physician was to heal and renew. He placed the Sabbath law where it belongs. And He abrogated the petty, man-made rules that abolished the spiritual intent of the Law.

In Mark 2:23–28 Jesus reminded the Pharisees of David's use of the Sabbath when he was in need. (Certainly the Levitical priests themselves did necessary work on the Sabbath—changing the shewbread, trimming the lamps, and burning incense.) On another occasion Jesus asked who would not lead his ox to water on the Sabbath (Luke 13:15). He also pointed to circumcision as the most pronounced relaxation of the Sabbath law: "If a man on the sabbath day receive circumcision, that the law of Moses should not be broken, are ye angry at me, because I have made a man every whit whole on the sabbath day?" (John 7:23). Jesus summed up His teaching on the subject: "The sabbath was made for man, and not man for the sabbath. Therefore, the Son of man is Lord also of the sabbath" (Mark 2:27–28).

Sabbath Services in the Jewish Home

The Sabbath is the oldest and most honored of all Jewish holy days. The Sabbath is kept sacred for two reasons: first, as a memorial to the creation of the world (Exod. 20:11); second, as a memorial to the Exodus of Israel from Egyptian bondage (Deut. 5:15). The Sabbath is an unhurried, home-centered holy day, complete with food and wine as a token of joy and festivity. The beautiful and meaningful Sabbath services in Jewish homes follow this pattern:

1. Twenty minutes before sundown on Friday, the wife or mother lights the Sabbath candles. One candle is symbolic of the "remembrance of the Sabbath" (Exod. 20:8); the other is symbolic of the "observance of the Sabbath" (Deut. 5:12).

2. The benediction is then recited over the candles, "Blessed art Thou, Lord our God, King of the

universe, who has sanctified us with His commandments and commanded us to kindle the Sabbath
lights." Then each member of the household greets
the others with *Sabbat shalom*, Sabbath peace.

3. The father then blesses the children. With his hands
    on his son's head, he says, "May God make you as
    Ephraim and Manasseh." Then with his hands on
    his daughter's head, he says, "May God make you
    as Sarah, Rebecca, Rachel, and Leah."

4. The father then raises the *kiddush* cup, full of wine,
    and recites the *kiddush* (sanctification) of the day.
    The wine must be grape-*kosher* wine or nonfer-
    mented, natural, *kosher* grape juice. Two loaves of
    Hallah (twisted Sabbath bread) are kept covered.

5. Everyone then ritually washes their hands. The
    hand benediction is then recited, "Blessed art Thou,
    Lord our God, King of the universe, who has
    sanctified us with His commandments and com-
    manded us concerning the washing of hands."

6. The loaves of *Hallah* are uncovered, and lifting
    them, the father says, "Blessed art Thou, Lord our
    God, King of the universe, who brings forth bread
    from the earth." The bread is then cut and distrib-
    uted. The cloth covering the loaves of *Hallah* sym-
    bolizes the dew that lay over the manna provided in
    the wilderness, and the two loaves themselves
    symbolize the double portion of manna God gave
    the Israelites for the Sabbath (Exod. 16:22).

The Sabbath is concluded when one can see the first three stars Saturday night. The *Havdalah* (farewell) to the Queen Sabbath is then recited. The purpose of this service is to separate the holy from the profane, the Sabbath from the ordinary.

1. The *Havdalah* is recited over a cup of wine filled to the brim.

2. The *Havdalah* candle (only one), which has braided wicks, is lit to demonstrate that the first act of the week is to make light, just as God's first creative act was to make light.

3. A special spice box containing cloves, cinnamon, nutmeg, and bay leaf is blessed and passed to each person to smell. The rabbis said that the sweetness of the spices delights the soul, reminding the participants of the sweetness of Queen Sabbath until the next Sabbath.

4. The participants then look at their hands in the light and say the concluding prayer, "Blessed art Thou, Lord our God, King of the universe, who makes a division between the sacred and the secular, between light and darkness, between Israel and the other nations, between the seventh day and the six working days. Blessed art Thou, Lord, who makes a distinction between the sacred and the secular."

But who is Queen Sabbath's counterpart king? Who is the bridegroom? The Jewish mystics believed he would be the Messiah-King. In their view the messianic age would be "all Sabbath and rest in life everlasting" (Mishnah, Tamid, 7:4). While the Sabbath was considered queen to God's King Messiah, she was considered bride to Israel the bridegroom. Note how close this Jewish concept comes to the New Testament teaching. Jesus is the Messiah-King-Bridegroom, the "Lord of the Sabbath," according to the New Testament. He will ever be the crown of the Torah's teaching about the Sabbath.

THE DIETARY LAWS

The Torah stated, "I am the LORD your God: ye shall therefore sanctify yourselves . . . to make a difference between the unclean and the clean, and between the beast that may be eaten and the beast that may not be eaten" (Lev. 11:44, 47).

The Torah's dietary laws were directed toward taking and eating animal life. The laws clearly indicated for the Jews which meats were proper or fit (*kosher*) for consumption. Almost more than any other part of the Mosaic law, the dietary laws (*kashrut*) distinguished Israel from other nations and marked them as a holy or separated people.

During the time of Jesus, rabbinical tradition included a vast number of supplementary regulations to the dietary laws of Moses. Because the rabbis taught that certain foods in themselves polluted the soul, many scribes became preoccupied with the dietary laws relating to ceremonial defilement. In fact, over a period of 2,500 years, the rabbis became so occupied with making decisions on dietary rules that the laws of *kashrut* became a serious area of specialized study.

Ritual defilement concerned the Pharisees greatly. Such matters as washing the hands before meals a certain number of times and in a certain way became law. If one did not follow the prescription, that person could be considered defiled. Rabbi Akiba ben Joseph once said, "He that takes meat with unwashen hands is worthy of death." Yet, Moses gave no such directive. The rules about washing were the elders' refinement of the Torah.

Jesus did not quarrel with the Torah's dietary laws. Undoubtedly He never ate pork or shellfish. But He taught that abstinence from certain foods did not make a person truly *"kosher"* or "religious." Jesus pointed out that the only defilement was inward, spiritual and moral, as evidenced by what came out of the person. He explained to His disciples, "Do not ye yet understand, that whatsoever entereth in at the mouth goeth into the belly, and is cast out into the draught? But those things which proceed out of the mouth come forth from the heart; and they defile the man. For out of the heart proceed evil thoughts, murders, adulteries, fornications, thefts, false witness, blasphemies. These are the things which defile a man; but to eat with unwashen hands defileth not a man" (Matt. 15:17–20). In the new age of the Messiah, the dietary laws still stand as matters of good hygiene, health, and medical wisdom, but no longer can they be considered matters of spiritual religion.

Kashrut in Jewish Life

A Jewish sage has said, "The numerous laws which regulate the eating habits of the Jew are purposed to test his holiness and his love for God." According to Jewish tradition, the dietary laws were not given merely for hygienic purposes. A horse can be as clean as a cow, but a horse is still *terefah* (unfit). A camel can be as nutritious as a goat, yet a camel is still *terefah*. A pig can be as free from disease as a sheep, but a pig is still *terefah*, according to the Torah.

The observant Jew adheres to the laws of *kashrut* because God said certain animals could be eaten and other animals could not (Lev. 11). Observance of the dietary laws were to mark Israel as a distinct and holy people (Lev. 11:44). The Jew would say that the laws of *kashrut* are a diet for the soul. They are intended more for spiritual well-being than for physical well-being.

The Torah declared that only *kosher* animals were fit to be offered to the Lord on the altar; *terefah* animals were prohibited. The Talmud suggests the transition from Old Testament sacrifices to today's world: "When the temple stood, sacrifices would secure atonement for an individual; now his table does" (Hag. 27a). This teaching implies that since the altar is no longer standing in the temple court, the table of the observant Jew now serves as an altar. Therefore, what is put on the table and what is eaten must be *kosher*. The ritual blessing at the table, sprinkling salt on the first bite of bread, removal of knives (weapons of war and violence), and the table where the food is eaten are all symbolic of an offering to the Lord.

Under certain conditions even a "clean" animal can become *terefah*. If a cow was diseased when it was slaughtered, if the slaughter was not *kosher*, if any blood was left after draining, if the cow had died from an accident, or if it had aged too long, then the cow would be *terefah*, unfit for consumption.

Although Moses never gave details for the practice of the slaughter of animals, the Oral Torah handed down many strict rules governing the ritual slaughter of animals (*shehitah*). All slaughtering is to be done only by the *shohet*, who must be a pious Jew, obedient to the Torah. He is given his credentials by the rabbis who make sure he properly kills the animals under the laws of *kashrut*. Rules that the *shohet* follows include:

1. The meat must belong to the right species—a cow, for example.

2. It must be slaughtered by a *shohet*, who also offers the proper ritual prayers.

3. It must be slaughtered with a *kosher* knife, which cannot be dented, nicked, or bent.

4. The animal cannot be stunned first.

5. With a fast stroke of the knife, the jugular veins, trachea, esophagus, the two carotid arteries, and the two vagus nerves are severed—without pain to the animal. Death is instant.

6. The animal must be thoroughly drained of blood.

7. The organs must be examined for disease.

8. The hind quarters are forbidden because the sciatic nerves contain many blood vessels that are almost impossible to remove.

When the meat is prepared at home, it must be soaked for half an hour, sprinkled with *kosher* salt, and given another hour for the blood to drain; then it must be rewashed under cold running water. The meat must not be cooked in "blood drippings," and it cannot be cooked in a utensil used for dairy products. In fact, meat and dairy products can neither be cooked together nor eaten together. A pious Jew will not eat dairy products within six hours of eating meat.

Reasons for the *Kashrut* Requirements

There are mixed reasons for the strict *kashrut* laws within the Jewish community:

1. They help to curtail cultural relationships between Jews and Gentiles. Dietary laws definitely separate.

2. They portray the Jews as a people dedicated to their religious convictions.

3. They are intended to help Jews maintain ritual holiness.

4. They designate the Jews as a people elected for God's service.

5. They help the Jews to retain Jewish identity.

6. In view of a pleasure-seeking world, which is often idolatrous, they help the Jews to maintain moral discipline.

7. They have contributed to Jewish cultural cohesiveness because Jews have had to live together to make available *kosher* foods, which they could not get outside the ghetto.

But today Jews face problems if they wish to live under *kashrut* rules. Some Jews believe that these dietary laws have no place in modern life. Others believe that the laws are the remains of a primitive society. Perhaps the more real problem is that a *shohet* is sometimes hard to find. Imported *kosher* foods are also hard to find. Getting out of the ghetto makes it difficult for a Jew to keep *kosher* in our mobile society.

THE LAW OF THE SANCTUARY

The Torah stated, "Unto the place which the LORD your God shall choose out of all your tribes to put his name there, even unto his habitation shall ye seek, and thither thou shalt come" (Deut. 12:5). In the time of Moses "the place of God's name" was the tabernacle. When the pillar of fire by night and the pillar of cloud by day stopped guiding Israel, the tabernacle was pitched, and the "habitation" of the Lord was set up. During the time of Solomon, the habitation of the Lord was the temple in Jerusalem, the most permanent place God had yet chosen to put His name.

In the days of Jesus (after Solomon's temple was destroyed in 586 B.C.), the place of God's name was the second temple, built in 516 B.C. and rebuilt in 20 B.C. by Herod. Erected on Mount Moriah in Jerusalem, the temple was the central sanctuary and the house of God. To this temple the devoted brought their vows, tithes, prayers, offerings, sacrifices, and worship. To honor the Torah was to honor the temple, and to honor the temple was to honor God.

Herod's temple was a magnificent structure. Greco-Roman in facade, it was made of polished granite. Its double porticoes of 162 Corinthian columns of white marble were overlaid with gold. The Talmud said, "Whoever did not see the temple of Herod missed seeing the most beautiful building in the world."

When Jesus walked the earth, the temple was controlled by the Sadducean party. It was the party of the high priest Caiaphas who ruled from A.D. 18 to 36. Under his rule and influenced by his predecessor, Annas, the Sadducees sought political power over religious purity. They readily allowed vested interests to corrupt the sanctity of the Lord's Court.

The heart of temple commercialism was the money-changing business. While the Torah laid down the requirement for every man to pay a yearly shekel tax to the temple, it was the Talmud that instructed in changing money: "It is necessary that everyone should have a half shekel to pay for himself. Therefore, when he comes to the exchange to change a shekel for two half shekels he is obliged to allow the money-changer some gain."

However, money-changers in the temple were not charging a small fee; they were fleecing the Passover pilgrims by an exorbitant rate. Avoiding the money-changers was difficult because all Roman coinage as well as shekels had to be exchanged for half shekels.

Inspectors of sacrificial animals also defrauded the pilgrims by rejecting animals brought from home or bought outside the temple, thereby forcing the offerers to buy "approved" animals from temple traders at an unfair price. The central sanctuary was further profaned by traders carrying their stock through it, using it as a short cut. The noise and smells in the court of the Gentiles made prayer impossible for devoted worshipers.

Jesus supported the temple in more than mere sentiment. He paid the temple tax (Matt. 17:24–27) as instructed in the Torah. He spent much of His time worshiping and teaching there. But because of His love for the temple, His concern for purity, and His faithfulness to the Torah, Jesus became angry over the sacrilege of the house of God. Turning over tables and thrusting out the merchants, "[he] would not suffer that any man should carry any vessel through the temple" (Mark 11:16). The prophet Malachi said: ". . . and the Lord, whom ye seek, shall suddenly come to his temple, even the messenger of the covenant, whom ye delight in; behold, he shall come, saith the LORD of hosts. But who may abide the day of his coming? And who shall stand when he appeareth? For he is like a refiner's fire, and like fullers' soap" (Mal. 3:1–2).

With righteous anger Jesus cleansed the temple and declared His judgment, "Is it not written, My house shall be called of all nations the house of prayer? But ye have made it a den of thieves" (Mark 11:17).

THE LAW OF THE LEPER

The Torah said,

> This shall be the law of the leper in the day of his cleansing: He shall be brought unto the priest; and the priest shall go forth out of the camp, and the priest shall look; and, behold, if the plague of leprosy be healed in the leper, Then shall the priest command to take for him that is to be cleansed two birds alive and clean, and cedar wood, and scarlet, and hyssop; And the priest shall command that one of the birds be killed in an earthen vessel over running water. As for the

living bird, he shall take it, and the cedar wood, and
the scarlet, and the hyssop, and shall dip them and the
living bird in the blood of the bird that was killed over
the running water. And he shall sprinkle upon him
that is to be cleansed from the leprosy seven times,
and shall pronounce him clean, and shall let the living
bird loose into the open field.

(Lev. 14:2–7)

The term *Cara'ath* in the Hebrew text, translated "lepra"
in Greek, did not always mean the loathsome disease that
permanently disfigured and resulted in death. Ancient
Hebrews used the term to designate many skin diseases.
But leprosy, as we know it, was covered by the Greek
word "lepra."

God appointed the Levitical priests to be the first
"health inspectors" among His ancient people. It was the
priests' job to distinguish between the contagious and the
noncontagious. If a priest declared a person unclean with
malignant leprosy, that man or woman was expected to
go about as a mourner with torn clothes and unkempt
hair, proclaiming a warning "unclean, unclean," to those
in the healthy community.

When the priest pronounced a leper healed, he would
take the restored leper to a place of running water for the
ceremonial cleansing described in Leviticus. The Torah
also required the healed leper to bring a guilt offering, a
burnt offering, and a cereal offering after eight days. The
priest then touched an ear, thumb, and toe of the
cleansed person with the blood of the guilt offering and
with oil.

In Jesus' healing ministry, He encountered several
lepers:

> *And there came a leper to him, beseeching him, and*
> *kneeling down to him, and saying unto him, If thou*
> *wilt, thou canst make me clean. And Jesus, moved*
> *with compassion, put forth his hand, and touched*
> *him, and saith unto him, I will; be thou clean. And as*
> *soon as he had spoken, immediately the leprosy*
> *departed from him, and he was cleansed. And he*
> *straitly charged him, and forthwith sent him away;*
> *and saith unto him, See thou say nothing to any man:*
> *but go thy way, show thyself to the priest, and offer*
> *for thy cleansing those things which Moses com-*
> *manded, for a testimony unto them.*
>
> (Mark 1:40–44)

The man in this encounter had already been pronounced "unclean" by the priest. His malignant leprosy
was the most horrible of diseases to look upon. But
probably his greater grief was caused by his defilement
under the Torah. Total isolation, often accompanied by
near starvation, utter social rejection, and inevitable death
were the miserable lot of this leper. Besides his other
suffering, the leper faced terrible guilt since the Jews
believed his condition was the result of some sin in his
family line.

Jesus showed remarkable compassion for the leper. He
did not drive the man away because he had violated the
Torah (Lev. 13:45). Instead He reached out and touched
the leper, apparently violating the Torah. Or did He? If
there was a possibility of spreading the disease, He was
certainly a lawbreaker. But in healing the disease, He was
free to verify His power. According to the Torah, the
priest alone was allowed to lay his hands on the tainted
skin and pronounce the leper cleansed. But with His

healing touch, Messiah proved Himself to be a priest of a higher order (Heb. 5:5–6). Having cleansed the leper, Jesus kept the Law by sending him to the priest for examination, certification, and the sacrificial bird offering required by the Torah.

THE LAW'S CREED

For the Jews, the heart of the Torah was: "Hear, O Israel: The LORD our God is one LORD: And thou shalt love the LORD thy God with all thine heart, and with all thy soul, and with all thy might" (Deut. 6:4–5).

This primary confession of faith was designated the *Shema* from the first word "hear" in Hebrew. Pious Jews recited the *Shema* every morning and evening. They declared it in the services of the synagogues. Through it worshipers were directed to Yahweh (rendered LORD in the English text) and diverted from the many gods worshiped by surrounding nations. The *Shema* was the preamble to the Ten Commandments, and the Jews viewed it with greater reverence since, without it, they would fail the rest of the Law.

The Jewish sages clung to the creed of the *Shema* because they viewed it as a great summation of the law of Moses. They loved to make aphorisms, condensing the Torah to its common denominator, the heart of religion. They also made numerous distinctions in the commandments. The sages called some commandments "light" or "little," others "weighty" or "great." According to the rabbis' estimation, some of the commandments must be greater than others, and one or two would be "greatest." Many rabbis contended that the greater commandments dealt with sacrifice, and others dealt with circumcision.

The Talmud acknowledged 613 commandments, of which 365 were negative and 248 positive. One rabbi said that Moses gave 613 commandments, but David reduced them to 11 (Ps. 15:2–5); Isaiah reduced them further to 6 (Isa. 33:15); Micah to 3 (Mic. 6:8); Amos to 2 (Amos 5:4); and Habbakuk to 1 (Hab. 2:4). (This last one, "the just shall live by his faith," was Paul's spiritual appeal in the Book of Romans.)

One of the rabbis' favorite methods for condensing the truth of the Torah was to connect unrelated passages in a summation paragraph. Several teachers had connected the *Shema* with Leviticus 19:18, ". . . thou shalt love thy neighbor as thyself: I am the LORD." In fact, Rabbi Hillel the Elder, who lived a generation before Jesus, had constructed a kind of "golden rule" based on the idea: "And what is hateful to you, do not do to your fellow man." Hillel added, "The rest of the Torah is merely commentary."

Jesus used this method of condensing and combining verses to simplify the Torah:

> *And one of the scribes came, and having heard them reasoning together, and perceiving that he had answered them well, asked him, Which is the first commandment of all? And Jesus answered him, The first of all the commandments is: Hear, O Israel: The Lord our God is one Lord; And thou shalt love the Lord thy God with all thy heart, and with all thy soul, and with all thy mind, and with all thy strength: this is the first commandment. And the second is like, namely this: Thou shalt love thy neighbor as thyself. There is none other commandment greater than these.*
> (Mark 12:28–31)

Jesus was so well versed in the Torah, He immediately appealed to the *Shema* in describing the greatest commandment. In doing so, He confirmed the *Shema* as capstone of the Torah. But He also combined the love of neighbor with love of God in classic rabbinic style. His answer to the scribe was not only a reflection of His own piety but also an indication of His profound insight and understanding of the Law. Jesus did not merely verbalize the *Shema*; He practiced it every day of His life.

The Jewish *Shema*

Every observant Jew must recite the *Shema* twice a day, morning and evening, as described in the precept, "Thou shalt . . . talk of them . . . when thou liest down, and when thou risest up" (Deut. 6:7). *Shema* is not a prayer but a declaration of Israel's faith. Without a doubt the oldest continual creedal statement ever voiced, the *Shema* is psychologically powerful as it reminds every Jew of the signs of the covenant made at Sinai as well as the individual obligation to God. To indicate reverence for the *Shema*, every observant Jew wears a head covering when it is recited.

Following the commands in Deuteronomy 6:8–9 to "bind them [the commands] for a sign upon thine hand . . . and . . . write them upon the posts of thy house and on thy gates," Jews have included portions of the *Shema* in their *mezuzahs* and in their *tephillin*. The *mezuzah* is a small case attached to the right side of the doorframe of a Jewish home. In it are placed the words from Deuteronomy 6:4–9 and Deuteronomy 11:13–21. The *tephillin* are leather boxes worn on the forehead and left arm during prayer.

LAW OF THE TASSELS

The Torah said, "Speak unto the children of Israel, and bid them that they make them fringes in the borders of their garments throughout their generations, and that they put upon the fringe of the borders a ribband of blue: And it shall be unto you for a fringe, that ye may look upon it, and remember all the commandments of the LORD, and do them" (Num. 15:38–39).

God instructed the Israelites to be a people different from their neighbors even in dress. According to the Torah, the men were to make tassels tied with blue ribbon for the four corners of their outer garments. The tassel was not to be merely a badge of national identity, like Scotch plaid, but a memorial of God's commandments.

The tasseled Israelite was a "marked" man in his own eyes and in the eyes of others. The tassels reminded him of his relationship to God, the Torah, and his national heritage. The blue ribbon that bound each tassel was meant to remind him of heaven and the God of heaven. The tassels themselves consisted of four threads that passed through a hole at the four corners of the outer garment. The four threads doubled to make eight. One of the threads was longer and was twisted seven times around the others and into a double knot, then eight times, then eleven times, then thirteen times. The first three numbers equaled twenty-six, the numerical value of the name of God, which was never pronounced among the Jews. The remaining number, thirteen, equaled the numerical value of the letters in the Hebrew word, "One," the last word in the *Shema*. Together the numerical equivalent was 613, representing all the laws in the Torah.

In obedience to the Torah, Jesus wore the required tassels (*tzitzit*, meaning "blossom") on His outer garment. Undoubtedly the special hem of tassels was referred to in Matthew 9:20–22: "And, behold, a woman, which was diseased with an issue of blood twelve years, came behind him, and touched the hem of his garment; For she said within herself, If I may but touch his garment, I shall be whole. But Jesus turned him about, and when he saw her, he said, Daughter, be of good comfort; thy faith hath made thee whole. And the woman was made whole from that hour."

When the woman reached for the tassels on Jesus' outer garment, she sought the holy ornaments. As she touched them, she felt healing (Mark 5:29). But partly to correct any superstition that healing came through the tassels themselves, Jesus turned and said, "Thy faith hath made thee whole." He called her "daughter," transferring her from ceremonial defilement and ostracism under the Law to wholeness in His kingdom.

The Jewish Garment for Prayer

> Blessed art Thou, Lord our God, King of the universe, who has sanctified us with His commandments and commanded us to wrap ourselves in the *tzitzit*.

Every Jewish male says this blessing each day before morning prayer, before he wraps himself in his prayer shawl (*tallit*). While standing, the observant Jew will hold his *tallit* in both hands and recite the blessing.

When a boy is thirteen and ready for *Bar Mitzvah*, he will be given a *tallit* as a gift to wear during morning prayer. It is never used on the Sabbath, in keeping with the commandment not to carry or be encumbered with anything on that day.

The *tallit* is really a modification of the Torah's instruction to wear a garment with tassels. It is a four-cornered shawl containing four tassels (*tzitzit*). During the recitation of the *Shema*, the four tassels are brought together and kissed during the reading of the third paragraph.

For the Jew today, as centuries ago, the tassels are reminders of the duty to the Torah. Modern rabbinic law no longer requires that the garment be worn publicly but only in home and synagogue use.

The *tallit* is impressively adorned with solid blue or black bands, reminders of perpetual lamentation over the destruction of the temple. No matter what color or how elaborate, the shawl is secondary to the purpose of the tassels. The Orthodox Jew wears a *tallit* reaching to the ankles; a Conservative Jew wears a short modification of the *tallit*; and the Reformed Jew has discontinued the use altogether.

THE LAW OF PHYLACTERIES

The Torah stated, "And it shall be for a token upon thine hand, and for frontlets between thine eyes; for by strength of hand the LORD brought us forth out of Egypt" (Exod. 13:16).

After Moses received the Law and before the scribes and their writing materials became abundant, few written copies of the Torah existed. Only at the Feast of Tabernacles every seven years did the Israelites hear it read completely. Therefore, God instructed the men of Israel to write portions of it, presumably on bits of parchment or cloth material, and wear the Scriptures around their wrists and heads. He also directed families to attach sections of the Torah on the walls of their homes or over their front doors. Though the entire Torah was not available to the common people, they could at least see and meditate on certain important sections.

Although God's intention in the practice was spiritual—to aid the Jews in keeping the Word of God in heart and mind—the literal practice of writing bits of Scripture and placing them on forehead and arm became a custom among the Jews. Even when copies of the Torah began to multiply and circulate, the Israelites retained the custom as a mark of personal piety. The use of the *tephillin* eventually was regulated under the 160 rules of Written Law.

The band of Scripture worn on head and arm came to be called *tephillin*, meaning "prayer" or "prayer bands," because most Jews wore them principally during prayer. Phylacteries, or *tephillin*, were small, cube shaped, leather boxes tied to the head and upper left arm by leather bands. Sewed into the boxes were four portions of the Torah centering on the purpose of the *tephillin* (Exod. 13:1–10, 16; Deut. 6:4–8; 11:13–21).

The Jews believed that the placement of the *tephillin* was symbolic. The Word of God was a memorial worn on the hand or arm, the instrument of action, and around the head, the organ of thought. Some rabbis believed that wearing a band on the head caused God's radiance to shine on the wearer and protected him from evil. One rabbi said, "God Himself wears *tephillin*." Another believed that by wearing the *tephillin*, he would live longer. Rabbi Eliezer said when one wore *tephillin*, God considered him as having studied the Torah day and night.

Neither the Torah nor oral tradition prescribed the size of phylacteries, but according to Jesus in Matthew 23:5, some of the Jewish enthusiasts made them unnecessarily broad: "But all their works they do for to be seen of men; they make broad their phylacteries, and enlarge the borders of their garments." Not only did Jesus denounce the extravagant size of some of the *tephillin* worn by the Pharisees, but His use of the word "phylactery" also implied a criticism of their spiritual understanding. The word He chose comes from the Greek word meaning "guard," suggesting the idea of a charm or amulet. Some Jews had actually come to view the phylacteries as "good luck charms" or a superstitious protection from evil. Jesus did not denounce the proper use of *tephillin*. It is conceivable that on occasion He wore phylacteries as an observant Jew following the customs of His people. Certainly He did not need boxes of Scripture portions to remind Him of God's Word. The Torah was inscribed on His heart. But Jesus condemned religious externalism and, as always, He clung to the intent of the Torah's laws about *tephillin*.

The ritualistic procedure for putting on the *tephillin* is precise:

1. Women are exempt from using the *tephillin*.

2. Boys start using them continually at age thirteen.

3. The *tephillin* are kissed before they are put on.

4. The *tephillin* are put on while a person is standing.

5. The hand (arm) *tephillin* is put on first. It is placed on the left biceps, next to the heart.

6. Before tightening the *tephillin*, the blessing is recited:

    "Blessed art Thou, Lord our God, King of the universe, who has sanctified us with His commandments and commanded us to put on *tephillin*."

7. The straps are then wound around the arm toward the body seven times and around the palm. (Seven times because the covenant is to be remembered each day of the week.)

8. The head *tephillin* is then put on. Before tightening it, the blessing is recited:

    "Blessed art Thou, Lord our God, King of the universe, who has sanctified us with His commandments and commanded us concerning the mitzvah of *tephillin*."

9. When the *tephillin* is firmly fixed, the blessing is recited:

    "Blessed be He whose glorious majesty is forever and ever."

    The *tephillin* is placed exactly between the eyes, but not below the hairline. It is to rest on the head, next to the brain.

10. The straps are left hanging down each side of the chest.

11. The strap around the palm is unwrapped and wound three times around the middle finger. The rest of the strap is carried around the ring finger and wound around the palm.

12. Finally, Hosea 2:19–20 is recited:

> "I will betroth thee unto me forever; yea, I will betroth thee unto me in righteousness, and in judgment, and in loving-kindness, and in mercies. I will even betroth thee unto me in faithfulness: and thou shalt know the LORD."

Today the *tephillin* are worn only during morning prayer, but years ago, according to the Talmud, they were worn all day.

Chapter 6

THE TORAH'S FESTIVAL CELEBRANT

Scripture for study:

> *And the* Lord *spake unto Moses, saying, Speak unto the children of Israel, and say unto them, Concerning the feasts of the* Lord, *which ye shall proclaim to be holy convocations, even these are my feasts. . . . These are the feasts of the* Lord, *even holy convocations, which ye shall proclaim in their seasons:*
>
> (Lev. 23:1–2, 4)

> *And now his [Christ's] parents went to Jerusalem every year at the feast of the passover. And when he was twelve years old, they went up to Jerusalem after the custom of the feast.*
>
> (Luke 2:41–42)

Celebration was a recurring theme of the Torah. Since Israel had known no holidays, festivals, or vacations in Egypt, God decreed days and seasons for enjoyment and reflection on the power and goodness of the Lord in delivering them from slavery (Lev. 23). The mighty acts of God were to be celebrated with remembrance and happiness.

The Hebrew calendar year was originally marked with seven yearly holy convocations or festivals. After the first giving of the Law, the celebrants came to the tabernacle for festival worship. Then, when Israel found permanent residence in Canaan, festivals were held in the nation's central sanctuary. During the intertestamental and New Testament periods, worshipers were scattered to their local synagogues. Passover and the Feast of Tabernacles were primarily home-centered feasts, but festival participants still gathered at the temple or synagogue as well.

According to Leviticus 23, Moses established the following festivals: Sabbath (the weekly celebration), Passover (Feast of Unleavened Bread), First Fruits, Pentecost, the Feast of Trumpets (New Year's Day), the Day of Atonement (a fast rather than a feast day), and the Feast of Tabernacles. Two more celebrations were added after Moses' instructions. The Feast of Purim commemorated the Jews' deliverance in Persia under Queen Esther. The Feast of Dedication (Hanukkah) was created during the intertestamental period to rejoice in the restoration of the temple after the sacrilege of Antiochus Epiphanes.

Although the feasts and holy days were primarily historical reminders of God's goodness in the past, they also foreshadowed the future. In fact, the highest purpose for the sacrificial system inherent in the feasts was to foreshadow the coming redemption—a redemption greater than Israel's physical release from Egyptian bondage. The ultimate purpose of the Torah was to prophesy Christ, His atoning death, His kingdom, and the new people of God.

While each festival was rich with symbolism pointing to God's past dealings with His people, the same symbolism often pointed to the future when He would complete His work with His people. As the Messiah celebrated the holy feasts, the past was remembered; in the Messiah Himself the signs of the future were fulfilled.

FEAST OF UNLEAVENED BREAD: PASSOVER (*PESAH*)

The Torah stated,

> *For I will pass through the land of Egypt this night, and will smite all the first-born in the land of Egypt, both man and beast; and against all the gods of Egypt I will execute judgment: I am the* LORD. *And the blood shall be to you for a token upon the houses where ye are; and when I see the blood, I will pass over you, and the plague shall not be upon you to destroy you, when I smite the land of Egypt. And this day shall be unto you for a memorial; and ye shall keep it a feast to the* LORD *throughout your generations; ye shall keep it a feast by an ordinance for ever.*
> (Exodus 12:12–14)

After the weekly Sabbath, the first annual celebration in the Jewish calendar was the Feast of Passover, or *Pesah* in Hebrew. It was also celebrated as the Feast of Unleavened Bread. The celebration occurred at twilight before the full moon in the month of Nisan (March-April). Arriving in the spring, the festival also marked the first barley harvest and the beginning of spring calving. The second day of Passover was called the Festival of First Fruits and involved bringing the fruit of the barley harvest to the Lord in sacrifice and thanksgiving (Exod. 23:19).

In the original Passover, Moses instructed each household to slay a perfect, male yearling lamb and apply the blood over the lintel (top of the doorway) and upon the doorposts with a bunch of hyssop (the marjoram plant). God had told him that the angel of death would "pass over" each home where the blood of the lamb was applied. Where no blood was applied, the oldest son would die that night. The Egyptians by and large refused the order, and their oldest sons died; but the Israelites who followed God's directions were spared.

After killing the lamb for their protection, the Hebrews roasted it with bitter herbs and later burned what they could not eat that night. Since God had told them, "Ye shall eat it in haste" (Exod. 12:11b) in preparation for their flight to Canaan, they served only unleavened bread. They tied up their long outer garments, and although staffs and sandals were customarily left outside, they ate with staff in hand and sandals on their feet.

The lamb was to be a perpetual reminder of the sacrifice that saved their lives. The unleavened bread, later called the bread of affliction, was a reminder of their hasty exodus from Egyptian bondage. The bitter herbs were a memorial of their former bitter slavery.

As they did with all Mosaic law, the Jewish philosophers later expanded the regulations dealing with the Feast of Passover to include many minor provisions. According to their Mishnah, the requirements of selecting the lamb on the tenth day of Nisan and painting the blood on the lintel and doorposts applied only to the original Passover and was not to be repeated. After the time of Solomon, the priests transferred much of the ceremony to the temple. They successively allowed three groups of families into the temple court to kill the lambs. The heads of the families slaughtered the lambs, and the priests caught the blood in basins and tossed it against the base of the altar. This process replaced the slaughter of lambs on the thresholds of homes and brushing blood around the doors. The rabbis taught that Passover lambs could be slaughtered anytime after noon and before sunset.

Also in preparation for the Sabbath, the rabbis commanded a ceremonial search for the leaven, based on Exodus 12:19a, "Seven days shall there be no leaven found in your houses." They viewed leaven as a symbol for that which corrupted or polluted, that which spread evil. Therefore, one who did not conform to the regulation to search out the leaven was "cut off," excluded from the family and nation of Israel. Some of the rabbis interpreted this to mean the violator was considered dead. Other rabbis ordered violators beaten with thirty-nine lashes.

Many regulations governed cooking and eating the Passover meal. The Mishnah said the lamb must be roasted on a pomegranate wood skewer, and the bitter herbs used in preparing the lamb could include peppermint, lettuce, dandelion, or chicory. The herb mixture was also used for dipping the unleavened bread, or *matzah*.

When eating the Passover meal, the Jews reclined to demonstrate their position as freed men. They blessed the food during or after the meal, rather than before, and the bread was broken and distributed with a blessing. The head of the family distributed the wine first and indicated the prospects for future Passovers together. The family usually ended the meal with a hymn of praise.

JESUS AND PASSOVER

According to the regulations of the Torah, Jesus kept Passover meticulously: "Now the first day of the feast of unleavened bread the disciples came to Jesus, saying unto him, Where wilt thou that we prepare for thee to eat the passover? And he said, Go into the city to such a man, and say unto him, The Master saith, My time is at hand; I will keep the passover at thy house with my disciples. And the disciples did as Jesus had appointed them; and they made ready the passover" (Matt. 26:17–19).

Both Matthew and Luke mentioned traditional elements in their accounts of Jesus' last Passover. Jesus and the disciples reclined at the meal (Matt. 26:20); Jesus blessed the cup (Luke 22:17) and then the bread; He broke the bread and distributed it with a blessing (Luke 22:19); He dipped the bread (Matt. 26:23); He indicated future prospects of celebrating Passover together (Matt. 26:29); and together, they sang a hymn of praise (Matt. 26:30).

But the Passover meal Jesus enjoyed with His disciples was more than a historical memorial; it was a predictive forecast. Jesus did not vary the traditional ceremony, but He introduced new meaning. He served the cup and the bread not only as memorials of God's lamb and the deliverance from slavery in Egypt but also as His own blood and body. By shedding His blood on Calvary, He became the sacrificial lamb, freeing those who accept His sacrifice from the slavery of sin. According to 1 Corinthians 5:7, "For even Christ, our passover, is sacrificed for us."

The foreshadowing of the Messiah as the Lamb was clearly laid out in the Old Testament. The Passover lamb was a one-year-old male, representing the Messiah's fresh maturity; it was without blemish, pointing to His immaculate birth and perfect righteousness; it was taken from the flock, showing Messiah's involvement with humanity. In all the requirements of the lamb, Jesus demonstrated His qualifications. John the Baptist cried out at the beginning of His ministry, "Behold the Lamb of God!" (John 1:36).

Not only did Jesus' life fulfill Jewish expectations of the coming lamb but His death met all requirements as well. Certainly He died as the lamb, the vicarious victim. Specifically He died in Jerusalem, the Lord's appointed site for the sacrifice. His bones were not fractured even on the Cross because the Passover lamb was not to have broken bones.

In keeping with tradition, Jesus probably celebrated the Passover meal before sundown on the fourteenth of Nisan or, in other words, the eve of Passover. If so, He was crucified on the very day that the Paschal lambs were slain, on the fourteenth of Nisan; the Lamb of God died late in the afternoon.

In many ways Jesus also fulfilled the symbolism of today's Passover celebration. While the lamb is reduced to a shankbone and the agricultural festival is abandoned, the modern Passover centers on the unleavened bread, or *matzah*. It is presented in a bag of three parts called a *matzah tash*. The middle *matzah* is broken, then distributed. Although the rabbis have offered many interpretations to the three-part *matzah*, the plausible explanation came from Jesus Himself, the second person of the Trinity, who said, "This is my body which is given for you" (Luke 22:19).

Jewish Passover Today

Passover comes in the spring and commences the first barley harvest and spring calving. In today's Jewish home both the agricultural feature and the Paschal Lamb are missing.

> Once a rabbi's son asked his father, "Father, what is it that makes atonement for the soul?"
>
> "Why it is the blood my son," as he quoted Leviticus 17:11.
>
> "Then why are there no sacrifices in our synagogues?" persisted the lad.
>
> The old rabbi confessed sadly that no sacrifices could be offered lawfully except at Jerusalem. Then said his son, "Father, we have no atonement!"*

Today Passover is observed by the removal and abstention from all products containing leaven. During Passover week only unleavened bread (*matzah*) is eaten. On the first two nights a special ritual meal, called the *Seder*, is held in each home. This ceremony tells the story of the first Passover in Egypt. The head of the Orthodox Jewish home, dressed in his *kittel* and a white cloth crown that depicts both purity and kingship over his home, leads the family in the ritual meal. He follows the order of the *Seder* as it is outlined in a beautifully decorated booklet called the *Haggadah*, which means "telling." He gives members of the family, especially children, an opportunity to respond.

*Walter B. Knight, *Three Thousand Illustrations for Christian Service* (Grand Rapids: Wm. B. Eerdmans Publishing Company, 1954), p. 219.

Preparation for Passover includes a thorough spring cleaning to remove all products containing leaven. This means that even pets that have been fed foods containing leaven must be sold. The products can be sold to a Gentile with the understanding that they will be bought back after Passover, but the sale must be a legitimate sale to meet the Jewish law. The Gentile can sell the products back to the former owner with a profit, or the Gentile can decide not to resell the products at all.

The night before the eve of Passover, the family attempts to find all hidden leaven and ceremonially searches the house with a candle, a feather, a wooden spoon, and a paper sack. All that is collected must be burned. The family then recites the ritual of nullification: "All leaven and all *hametz* that is in my possession, that I did not see and did not destroy, let it be null and ownerless as the dust of the earth."

The *Seder* ritual was embellished by Rabban Gamaliel in the late first century. He taught that each generation should imagine that it had just left Egyptian slavery. Each family, then, through the *Seder* ritual reenacts that first Passover. To help them remember each aspect of the Exodus, the *Seder* table is set with symbolic food:

1. Wine, the symbol of joy and festivity.

2. *Matzah*, the bread of affliction, the symbol of purity from evil.

3. Green vegetable, the symbol of spring productivity and joy.

4. Salt water, the symbol of tears.

5. Bitter herbs, the symbol of slavery.

6. Haroset (a mixture of ground apples, walnuts, cinnamon, and wine), the symbol of the brick mortar that the Israelite slaves made in Egypt.

7. An egg, the symbol of new life and resurrection.

8. Lamb shankbone, the symbol of the paschal lamb.

9. Large cup for Elijah, the symbol for the herald of Messiah.

Other ritual items include the traditional Sabbath candles, pillows to recline on, and the *matzah tash*, which is the three-sectioned bag cover into which the *matzah* is placed.

The order of the Passover *Seder* follows this pattern:

1. The *kiddush* cup of wine sanctifies the day.

2. The hands are washed.

3. The green vegetable is eaten.

4. The middle *matzah* is broken and is hidden for the *aphikoman*, the after dish.

5. The Passover story is recited.

6. The hands are washed again before the meal.

7. The blessing for the *matzah* is recited.

8. The bitter herb is eaten.

9. The bitter herb is eaten with *matzah*.

10. The festive meal is eaten.

11. The *aphikoman* is found and eaten.

12. The grace is offered after the meal.

13. The *Hallel* is recited.

14. The *Seder* is concluded.

Special characteristics of the *Seder* include the four questions asked by the youngest child:

1. "On all other nights we eat either leavened bread or unleavened bread; on this night why only unleavened?"

2. "On all other nights we eat herbs of any kind; on this night why only bitter herbs?"

3. "On all other nights we do not dip herbs even once; on this night why do we dip them twice?"

4. "On all other nights we eat our meals in any manner; on this night why do we sit around the table together in a reclining position?"

Another symbolic gesture is the drinking of the four cups of wine:

1. The cup of iniquity, reminding them of the plagues in Egypt.

2. The cup of praise.

3. The cup of blessing, also called the cup of redemption.

4. The cup of Elijah, also called the cup of acceptance.

One of the children opens the door for Elijah and everyone stands to greet him. The *Seder* is then concluded in anticipation: "Concluded is the Passover *Seder*, according to law and custom. As we have lived to celebrate it, so may we celebrate it again. O Pure One, who dwells in heaven above, restore the congregation of Israel in love. Speedily lead the offshoots of the stock redeemed, to Zion in joyous song. Next year in Jerusalem!"

FEAST OF WEEKS: PENTECOST (*SHAVUOT*)

The Torah stated,

> *And ye shall count unto you from the morrow after the sabbath, from the day that ye brought the sheaf of the wave offering; seven sabbaths shall be complete: Even unto the morrow after the seventh sabbath shall ye number fifty days; and ye shall offer a new meat offering unto the LORD. Ye shall bring out of your habitations two wave loaves of two tenth deals: they shall be of fine flour; they shall be baked with leaven; they are the firstfruits unto the LORD.*
>
> (Lev. 23:15–17)

On the second day of Passover, faithful Jews offered the first sheaves of the barley harvest to the Lord. They brought them to the temple in the Festival of First Fruits, a ceremony that made it clear that the first of everything, including all crops, belonged to God. The Festival of Weeks followed the offering of First Fruits by seven weeks or fifty days. It was called *Shavuot* in Hebrew, meaning "weeks," or Pentecost in Greek, meaning "fifty." The Feast of Weeks arrived at the end of wheat harvest and the beginning of fruit harvest. It was a joyous, religious celebration of ingathering, Israel's thanksgiving day. Through sacrificial gifts the nation expressed its dependence on God for future harvests.

Pentecost was an annual pilgrim festival, drawing crowds of people who brought gifts to the altar at Jerusalem. If the pilgrims came from nearby villages, they brought fresh figs and grapes. Those who came long distances brought dried dates, raisins, and figs. According to tradition, crowds often followed a sacrificial ox decorated with wreaths around its head. Music was a great part of the festival. As the pilgrims ascended Mount Zion, they were met by priests playing flutes. When the pilgrims reached Jerusalem, they were required to give two loaves of leavened bread of fine flour. The remaining sacrifices for Pentecost included seven lambs, one bullock, two rams, and a drink offering.

Today the agricultural nature of Pentecost has been phased out. The celebration now commemorates the seven-week pilgrimage of the Israelites from Egypt to Sinai and the receiving of the Law. Traditionally Jewish children begin their season in Hebrew school at this festival.

Apparently Jesus attended Pentecost as well as the

other pilgrim festivals. John 5:1 recorded, "After this there was a feast of the Jews, and Jesus went up to Jerusalem." The text implies a habitual pattern of journeying to Jerusalem three times a year for the feasts of Passover, Pentecost, and Tabernacles.

But Jesus did more than simply attend the feasts. In each case He was the fulfillment of festival symbolism. Just as He died on Passover while the lambs were being slaughtered and was buried on the Day of Unleavened Bread when the broken *matzah* was hidden, He arose from the dead on the Day of First Fruits when the first of the barley harvest was offered. As Paul later explained it, "But now is Christ risen from the dead and become the firstfruits of them that slept. For since by man came death, by man came also the resurrection of the dead. For as in Adam all die, even so in Christ shall all be made alive. But every man in his own order: Christ the firstfruits; afterward they that are Christ's at his coming" (1 Cor. 15:20–23). Christ was the first fruit of all who would come into His kingdom.

But fulfillment of the Torah's festivals did not stop with the Day of First Fruits. Fifty days after Christ's resurrection, He gave the Holy Spirit on the Day of Pentecost (Acts 2:1–41), specifically for an "ingathering" harvest of human souls to compose His church and kingdom. Possibly, the bread offering of Pentecost indicated further symbolism in the coming kingdom of Christ. The two loaves of leavened bread pointed to the two groups that would compose the new people of God. As the leaven indicated the sinful nature of the people (unlike Messiah who was symbolized by unleavened bread), the two loaves indicated a church composed of two major groups, Jews and Gentiles, taken from among the nations. Within

those two groups are many different cultural back-
grounds, but at His Pentecostal harvest they are forever
one redeemed people of God.

Jewish Pentecost Today

The rabbinic sages wished to give the ancient harvest
festivals higher religious meanings. They taught that in
essence, Passover was a forerunner or prelude to freedom. The rabbis believed that the Exodus was not total
liberation until the Jews received the Torah at Mount Sinai
seven weeks (fifty days) later. True freedom could come
only by receiving the blessing of the law of their God.
Thus today Pentecost, called "The Season of the Giving of
our Torah," commemorates the seven weeks from Egypt
to Sinai when the Law was revealed to Moses.

It has become traditional to start Jewish children in
Hebrew school during Pentecost. In keeping with the
theme, it presents a logical time for the first steps in the
study of the Torah. The rabbis would tell the children that
by studying the Torah, they would be standing side by
side with their forefathers, just as if they were standing
before the Lord at Mount Sinai. The festival has also
become a time for boys and girls to be confirmed.

In ancient times when a Jewish boy began studying the
Torah and the Hebrew alphabet, he was given a slate and
a mixture of flour and honey as chalk. He was told what
the letters were and how to pronounce them. After
instruction, the rabbi would point to a letter and say,
"What letter is that and how does it sound?" If the boy
answered correctly, he was allowed to lick the letter off
the slate as a reward. Pentecost taught that the law of the
Lord was sweet, as the psalmist said, "How sweet are thy

words unto my taste! yea, sweeter than honey to my mouth" (Ps. 119:103).

The Book of Ruth is read aloud in the synagogues during Pentecost. The book is ideal for the festival because it shows the devotion of a non-Jewish woman to Israel's God. The rabbis reasoned that if a non-Jew could show such faith in the God of Israel, then true Israelites should desire to renew their covenant to God during Pentecost.

Another characteristic of the festival is that Jews eat only dairy products during Pentecost. One would think that because of the agricultural origins of the festival, the people would eat cereals, fruits, and vegetables. But that was not the case. The people eat dairy products to symbolize that God directed their ancestors to a "land flowing with milk and honey."

FEAST OF TRUMPETS: NEW YEAR'S DAY (*ROSH HASHANA*)

The Torah stated,

> And the LORD spake unto Moses, saying, Speak unto the children of Israel, saying, In the seventh month, in the first day of the month, shall ye have a sabbath, a memorial of blowing of trumpets, an holy convocation. Ye shall do no servile work therein: but ye shall offer an offering made by fire unto the LORD."
>
> (Lev. 23:23–25)

Israel actually celebrated two New Year's Days. The first was in the first month of the year (Nisan), and it began the religious year with the observance of Passover.

The second was in the seventh month of the year (Tishri); it began the civil year with the Feast of Trumpets.

New Year's Day was a Sabbath day of rest. It was also a holy day of assembly for worship and a joyous celebration. Trumpets were the central feature of the New Year's festival. The day was summoned, not merely by the priest, but by all the people blowing ram's horns. They began blowing their trumpets at sunrise and continued until sundown.

One particular ram's horn was a signal for the harvesters working in the vineyards and grain fields to appear at the temple. The priest stood on the southwestern wall of the sanctuary to blow the horn for all in the neighboring fields to hear. At that moment those workers who were Jews laid down their tools, left their work, and immediately gathered at the temple.

The trumpet was a longstanding symbol of both joy and judgment to the Jews. The first mention of trumpets in the Torah was at the giving of the Law at Sinai (Exod. 19:13, 19). Throughout Israel's history the trumpets were blown to call assemblies (Num. 10:3); to announce the beginning of journeys (Num. 10:5, 6); to sound the alarm for war (Num. 10:9); to greet every new moon (Ps. 81:3); to praise God (Ps. 150:3); to proclaim the Year of Jubilee (Lev. 25:8–10); and to announce the time of sacrifices.

The Torah did not use the name Rosh Hashana. That phrase meaning "New Year" was introduced in the Mishnah by later rabbis. As with all the festivals, the leading rabbis added continually to the interpretation of the Feast of Trumpets as described in the Torah.

For Rosh Hashana the rabbis laid their greatest stress upon "remembering" at the blowing of the trumpets. They argued about exactly what to remember. Some said the trumpet was blown to remember God's grace to Abraham in delivering his son Isaac from sacrifice. Others said the trumpet was blown to remember God's creation of the world, which the rabbis believed occurred on the first week of the seventh month. One group thought the trumpet was blown to remind each person to repent and be ready for judgment. Others insisted the trumpet was blown to confuse Satan and drive him away. Yet another group said the trumpet was blown to remind God of His covenant with Israel.

Since Rosh Hashana preceded Yom Kippur (the Day of Atonement) by only ten days, many rabbis put the emphasis on repentance and taught that God gave Israel ten days to repent before the annual Day of Judgment. They said God opened three books on New Year's Day. The names of the righteous were recorded in the first. The names of those who were in "borderline" standing were inscribed in the second. The names of the wicked were found in the third. Thus on Rosh Hashana the people were to come before the Lord with fear and trembling as they faced the judgment.

JESUS AND THE FEAST OF TRUMPETS

Since Jesus lived under the Torah and was obedient to it, He undoubtedly celebrated the Feast of Trumpets with His people. Perhaps Jesus also blew the ram's horn many times in His life.

But as with the other festivals, He did more than merely celebrate the occasion. From His own experience with Rosh Hashana, He drew from the symbolism of the trumpet blast to describe His own second coming.

He said, "And then shall appear the sign of the Son of

man in heaven; and then shall all the tribes of the earth mourn, and they shall see the Son of man coming in the clouds of heaven with power and great glory. And he shall send his angels with a great sound of a trumpet, and they shall gather together his elect from the four winds, from one end of heaven to the other" (Matt. 24:30–31).

Just as the trumpet blast drew the faithful field workers to worship and left the others behind, so Jesus described the effect of the trumpet blast at His return. He said, "Then shall two be in the field; the one shall be taken, and the other left" (Matt. 24:40). He described angels as Messiah's attendants, blowing trumpets of judgment on that day. Paul also mentioned the last trumpet call to bring forth the dead to resurrection (1 Cor. 15:52; 1 Thess. 4:16). As the priests called their people to repentance and worship with the trumpets for Rosh Hashana, so Christ said the angels' blast will signal Christ's return and call God's assembly to pure worship and praise in glorious celebration of eternal jubilee.

Rosh Hashana Today

Rosh Hashana begins the ten days of awesome reflection and prayer before the Day of Atonement. The people listen to the sound of the ram's horn, the *shofar*, and remember that God is calling them to repentance. During the course of the service on Rosh Hashana, a total of one hundred notes is sounded. If a person is ill or infirm, the *shofar* is taken to them for sounding.

One of the symbolic foods for New Year's Day is an apple dipped in honey, suggesting that the new year may be as sweet as honey. The traditional wish is, "May it be the Lord's will to renew for us a year that will be good and sweet." The people greet each other with the traditional greeting, "May you be inscribed and sealed for a good year."

On the afternoon of Rosh Hashana, the people gather for a special service near a stream, river, or other body of water. Here they follow the injunction from Micah 7:19, "thou wilt cast all their sins into the depths of the sea" and shake their garments, portraying the casting off of sins for God to take away.

DAY OF ATONEMENT (YOM KIPPUR)

The Torah stated,

> *And the LORD spake unto Moses, saying, Also on the tenth day of this seventh month there shall be a day of atonement: it shall be a holy convocation unto you; and ye shall afflict your souls, and offer an offering made by fire unto the LORD. And ye shall do no work in that same day: for it is a day of atonement, to make an atonement for you before the LORD your God.*
> (Lev. 23:26–28)

The Torah demanded sacrifice for sin, and the Day of Atonement was the primary day of sacrifice. The talmudic commentary on the Day of Atonement (Yom Kippur) was entitled *Yoma*, meaning simply "the Day," revealing the importance of that day to the Jews. They viewed it as the most solemn of days, portraying two august facts: the sinfulness of humanity and the righteousness of God.

In Leviticus 16 Moses outlined the detailed procedure for sinful people to approach a holy God. The ritual for the *Yoma* followed this pattern:

1. Aaron bathed.

2. He put on white linen clothes.

3. He killed a bullock at the altar for himself and his household.

4. He brought incense within the veil of the Holy of Holies and burned it before the mercy seat.

5. He sprinkled the blood of the bullock on the mercy seat; before the mercy seat, he sprinkled the blood seven times with his finger.

6. He brought two goats to the door of the tabernacle.

7. He cast lots for the goats: one was the Lord's goat; one was the scapegoat.

8. He killed the Lord's goat as a sin offering for the people.

9. He reentered the Holy of Holies and sprinkled blood on the mercy seat and on the area in front of the mercy seat seven times (as before).

10. He then made atonement for the tabernacle and altar; he put the goat's blood on the horns of the altar and on all sides.

11. He placed his hands on the head of the living goat and confessed Israel's sins.

12. He sent the scapegoat into the wilderness.

13. He took off his linen clothes, leaving them in the tabernacle.

14. He bathed again.

15. He put on his regular priestly vestments.

16. He offered the fat for a burnt sin offering at the altar.

17. He ordered the residue of the bull and the goat to be taken out of camp and burned.

The painstaking steps required to satisfy a holy God taught an impressive and highly visible lesson every year. The Israelites clearly saw that removing transgressions involved a substitutionary, sacrificial atonement. God commanded Aaron to use two goats: one to pay for the sin, the other to remove the sin. God did not grant forgiveness because the sinners confessed their guilt or even because they desired mercy, but He forgave them because the goat had been sacrificed as a sin offering. The expiation was complete when Aaron sent the sins of the people into the wilderness on the head of the scapegoat.

Rabbinic tradition added to the already detailed regulations governing the Day of Atonement. According to the rabbis, the high priest was required to reside in a chamber of the temple apart from his private house for seven days before the day of sacrifice, in order to prepare himself for the awesome work ahead. During those seven days he performed the tasks of the common priests: trimming, cleaning, sacrificing. The work supposedly conditioned him in humble employment for his duties on the great Day. Traditionally the high priest repeatedly read and rehearsed the instructions and procedures to prevent any error.

The Jews also taught that the high priest must lay his hands on the head of the bullock before the sacrifice, confessing his own sins and those of his household. He then had to kill the animal with his own hands before he could make atonement for the congregation.

Jewish tradition further said that when the high priest entered the Holy of Holies, he had to walk in sideways to avoid looking directly at the mercy seat until it was covered with smoke from the incense. When he left the Holy of Holies, he was supposed to walk backward, expressing respect to the Divine Presence. After prayer he was to hurry out of the tabernacle to appear before the people, assuring them that he had not died in the presence of God and atonement had been made. After the ceremony the high priest's linen garments for that day were never worn again.

Although the Torah clearly directed the priest to send the scapegoat into the wilderness, later the priests began the custom of forcing the scapegoat over a cliff to be killed. The crowd made a pathway for the scapegoat, pulling its hair as it passed and saying, "Bear our sins and be gone!" The high priest accompanied the goat to a ravine. He then divided a crimson wool thread, tying one part to a rock and the other part to the goat's horns. He pushed the goat into the rocky ravine where it was often broken in pieces halfway down. A sentinel signalled the death of the goat, and the high priest returned to the people with the news, "The he-goat has reached the wilderness."

The Jews liked to say that if the scarlet wool tied to the rock turned white, Israel's sins were forgiven. For many years they reported that it did turn white. But according to their legend, for forty years before the temple's destruction in A.D. 70, the scarlet wool never changed to white. (Forty years before A.D. 70, Messiah had come to be the Atonement.)

JESUS AND THE DAY OF ATONEMENT

The Day of Atonement differed from the other religious celebrations in several ways. Unlike the home-centered celebrations, the Day centered on the work of the high priest. On the Day of Atonement, the Jews fasted rather than feasted. And unlike the repeated emphasis on thanksgiving and trust in God, Yom Kippur was a day of sorrow, repentance, and expiation of sin.

But more than any of the feast days, the Day of Atonement foreshadowed the work of Messiah. The writer of Hebrews described His fulfillment of that day:

> *For the law, having a shadow of good things to come and not the very image of the things, can never with those sacrifices which they offered year by year continually make the comers thereunto perfect. For then would they not have ceased to be offered? because that the worshipers once purged should have had no more conscience of sins. But in those sacrifices there is a remembrance again made of sins every year. For it is not possible that the blood of bulls and of goats should take away sins.*
>
> (Heb. 10:1–4)

Although the Jewish sacrifices availed to remove ceremonial impurity, they accomplished no permanent removal of sin. The repeated Levitical offerings presented
only a shadow of Christ's coming fulfillment as a sacrifice.
First, the animal victims were dragged unwillingly to the
altar. But Jesus voluntarily sacrificed Himself in loving
obedience to the Father. Second, the animal sacrifices
were inadequate to expiate the sins of the people. Bulls
and goats were incapable of spiritual suffering; they could
not vindicate God's justice. But Jesus not only offered a
physical sacrifice that was perfect, but He also offered it in
perfect obedience to God the Father. Jesus fulfilled the
roles of both the goat of sacrifice and the scapegoat. As
the goat of sacrifice, He was "without blemish," fulfilling
in perfect moral purity the requirements of the ceremonial
law and taking away the condemnation for sin. As the
scapegoat, He bore the sins of many: "So Christ was once
offered to bear the sins of many; and unto them that look
for him shall he appear the second time without sin unto
salvation" (Hebrews 9:28).

Yom Kippur Today

> All vows, bonds, oaths, devotions, promises,
> penalties, and obligations: wherewith we have
> vowed, sworn, devoted, and bound ourselves:
> from this Day of Atonement unto the next Day of
> Atonement, may it come unto us for good: lo, all
> these, we repent us in them. They shall be
> absolved, released, annulled, made void and
> none effect: they shall not be binding nor shall
> they have any power. Our vows shall not be
> vows; our bonds shall not be bonds; and our
> oaths shall not be oaths.

This *Kol Nidrei* prayer, offered on Yom Kippur, is perhaps the Jew's most sacred reflection. It reveals repentance and the inability to keep God's commandments. One tradition practiced on the eve of Yom Kippur, before the *Kol Nidrei* starts, is when the assembled worshipers stand and plead with their fellow Jews, "Hear, my masters! I plead forgiveness and pardon for all my offenses that I have committed against you in word or action."

Unlike the other festivals, Yom Kippur is a fast day. It is the most holy day of the year, a "Sabbath of Sabbaths," the Day of Judgment, a period of solemn introspection.

Since the destruction of the temple in A.D. 70 ended the Torah's requirement of animal sacrifice, the rite of *kapparah* was contrived to be a substitute. It is the practice of the very orthodox Jew to hold a chicken over the head, waving it three times and reciting, "This is my substitute; this is my commutation; the rooster goeth to death; but may I be gathered and enter into a long and happy life and unto peace." The ritual is intended to be a vicarious atonement for sins. The chicken is then ritually slaughtered by a *shohet* (the butcher). But this scapegoat chicken finds no support from the Torah. The less orthodox Jews have substituted gifts to charity for animal sacrifices.

Another custom, especially among eastern European Jewish communities, is the practice of *malka*, or stripes. The Torah commands that "you shall afflict your souls" (Lev. 23:27). Malka is practiced by adult male Orthodox Jews who, on the day before Yom Kippur, voluntarily submit to a beating of thirty-nine stripes. This attempt at self-atonement is also unsupported by the Torah.

Tradition says that the high priest went to the temple, entered the Holy of Holies on the Day of Atonement, and recited the confession of sins. To commemorate this action, today's congregation recites the litany of confession of sins, which mentions fifty-six types of sins. As the Jews recite each of the sins, they beat their chests with their right fists as a sign of sorrow. Though Jews do not normally kneel when they pray, Orthodox Jews make one full prostration in the temple on Rosh Hashana and four full prostrations on Yom Kippur.

The conclusion of Yom Kippur is marked in the synagogue by a single, long blast of the ram's horn, symbolic of the trumpet blast that concluded the revelation on Mount Sinai (Exod. 19:13). The trumpet blast is also a memorial of the *shofar* blown on the Day of Atonement in ancient Israel, marking the beginning of the Year of Jubilee.

The Torah states, "It is the blood that maketh an atonement for the soul" (Lev. 17:11). Atonement cannot come by repentance alone, charity, recitation of vows, study of Torah and Talmud, flagellation, or pool-side rituals. These all indicate an unsatisfied soul, craving to be made right with God. The New Testament says, "Without shedding of blood is no remission [of sins]" (Heb. 9:22). From the time animal sacrifices ceased, the sacrifice of Messiah was effective.

FEAST OF TABERNACLES: BOOTHS (SUCCOTH)

The Torah stated,

> *Also in the fifteenth day of the seventh month, when ye have gathered in the fruit of the land, ye shall keep a feast unto the LORD seven days. On the first day shall be a sabbath, and on the eighth day shall be a*

sabbath. And ye shall take you on the first day the boughs of goodly trees, branches of palm trees, and the boughs of thick trees, and willows of the brook; and ye shall rejoice before the LORD *your God seven days. And ye shall keep it a feast unto the* LORD *seven days in the year. It shall be a statute forever in your generations: ye shall celebrate it in the seventh month. Ye shall dwell in booths seven days; all that are Israelites born shall dwell in booths; That your generations may know that I made the children of Israel to dwell in booths, when I brought them out of the land of Egypt: I am the* LORD *your God.*

(Lev. 23:39–43)

The seventh month was the busiest season in the Hebrew year. The Feast of Trumpets introduced the seventh month as well as the civil New Year; ten days later came the Day of Atonement, and on the fifteenth day the joyous Feast of Tabernacles began.

The Feast of Tabernacles (or "Booths") memorialized Israel's wilderness journey and the temporary huts they lived in for forty years. The Hebrew name *Succoth* (meaning "booths" or "huts") referred to the Israelites' first encampment after leaving Egypt; at Succoth they experienced their first taste of freedom. For the Feast of Tabernacles the Jews constructed replicas of the huts or booths of their ancestors, and they lived in them for seven days. By remaining outdoors in the crude tabernacles, they relived some of the hardships of their ancestors. More important, they also rejoiced in the kind provision and protection of God.

Since the Feast of Tabernacles arrived at the end of the fruit harvest in the fall, it incorporated elements of a harvest celebration. The crops of grapes, olives, and other fruits had been picked before the celebration of the feast, so festival celebrants used the branches of their fruit trees and leafy palms to construct the booths.

A large number of sacrifices also characterized the feast. During the eight days of the festival, the priest offered seventy-two bullocks, fifteen rams, one hundred and five lambs, eight kids, and various meal and drink offerings. The priest presented the sacrifices in a diminishing order. In the case of the lambs, he offered fourteen lambs on the first day, diminishing one per day until he offered only one on the last day. With the bullocks he offered thirteen on the first day, diminishing to seven on the last day.

As with all the other feasts, rabbinic tradition added both regulations and interpretation to the Feast of Tabernacles. According to the rabbis, the seventy bullocks were a sacrifice for the seventy nations of the world who would one day come to know Israel's God. (According to some Christian interpreters, the diminishing sacrifices pointed to their eventual removal under the Messiah.)

Many rabbis turned their attention to constructing and living in booths, rather than to sacrifices. Rabbinic regulations specified that every Jew (except slaves, women, and small children) must dwell in huts, day and night, for the full seven days. The rabbis stressed the importance of abandoning social class for that week, reminding the participants of the Hebrew lessons about equality and justice.

The rabbis laid down exact details about the construction of the huts. They could not be higher than thirty feet nor less than four feet long and four feet wide. They were to be made with a roof of green boughs and constructed so that the dwellers could see the stars, just as their forefathers did in the wilderness. The huts were decorated inside with greenery, flowers, and fruits.

The Israelites developed another tradition for the Feast of Tabernacles by gathering citron (*ethrog*) and binding together the branches of palm, myrtle, and willow. Everywhere they went for the seven days, they carried the visible symbols of the celebration: citron in the left hand and bundles of branches (*lulav*) in the right. The palm spoke of victory; the willow indicated a happy, thriving condition; and the olive pointed to peace.

In later biblical times the tradition of the Water-Drawing Ceremony and Lighting Ceremony also developed (see chapter 7).

JESUS AND THE FEAST OF TABERNACLES

The Gospel said, "Now the Jews' feast of tabernacles was at hand. His brethren, therefore, said unto him, Depart hence, and go into Judea, that thy disciples also may see the works that thou doest. . . . But when his brethren were gone up, then went he also up unto the feast, not openly, but as it were in secret. . . . Now, about the midst of the feast, Jesus went up into the temple, and taught" (John 7:2–3, 10, 14).

As indicated by Jesus' family members in the above passage, they celebrated the Feast of Tabernacles under the Torah's requirements. Undoubtedly Jesus knew the experience of living under the green boughs of the hut during the traditional seven days. According to John's record, Jesus also journeyed to the sanctuary for the annual feast. He took the opportunity to teach in the temple.

But of all the celebrations that Jesus attended, the Feast

of Tabernacles was the one that most clearly pointed to His second coming as the triumphant king. Zechariah 14:16 directed the Jews toward a future Feast of Tabernacles that would draw all nations together in peace: "And it shall come to pass that every one that is left of all the nations which came against Jerusalem shall even go up from year to year to worship the King, the LORD of hosts, and to keep the feast of tabernacles." Because of Zechariah's prophecy, the Jews watched for a Messiah who would one day rule at the Feast of Tabernacles, and they kept their *lulavs* (bundles of branches) ready to wave in victory on that day.

When Jesus arrived in Jerusalem during His last week on earth, the crowds did briefly wave their *lulavs* with shouts of Hosanna, recognizing Christ as the Son of David and the rightful king. Although that celebration was short-lived, John later described a future, lasting celebration in the Revelation: "After this I beheld and, lo, a great multitude, which no man could number, of all nations, and kindred, and people, and tongues, stood before the throne, and before the Lamb, clothed with white robes, and palms in their hands" (Rev. 7:9). The crowd that John described was a future multitude of nations, celebrating the true prophetic Feast of Booths in the settled home of heaven.

Jewish Feast of Booths Today

Modern living has made the construction of booths difficult, especially for apartment dwellers. Therefore, many synagogues have erected their own community booths. In Jerusalem, a municipal shelter is provided for the entire city near the Jaffa gate.

In Yemen, the Feast of Tabernacles is such a popular and festive celebration that many of the Jews build their houses with one room as a permanent booth, leaving it without a ceiling. During the rest of the year, it is simply covered with mats to keep dust and rain out. During the festival, the booth is covered with green cactus and cornstalks since Yemen is a desert country. The people cover the floors with carpets and mats and hang myrtle leaves in the corners.

The Bukhuran Jews decorate their booths with splendid tapestries and colorful paper garlands. They cover the floor of the booth with thick carpet. In one corner they place "Elijah's chair," decorated with elaborate silks and supplied with holy literature, symbolizing a welcome to the prophet and the patriarchs. Tradition says that during the Feast of Tabernacles, the prophets and patriarchs visit the booths in spirit.

On the morning of the last day of the Feast of Tabernacles, called the Great Hosanna, the worshipers circle the synagogue seven times, carrying the *lulavs.* They then vigorously beat the *bimah* (platform) with the willows until all the leaves fall off. The rabbis said this symbolizes repentance, renewal of the soul, and the riddance of sins, just as the leaves drop off the trees in the fall and are renewed in the spring. A messianic prayer is then offered.

> Turn unto me and be ye saved, today if ye hear his voice. Behold the man who sprang forth— Branch is his name—David himself. Stand up! Be buried in the dust no longer! Ye who dwell in the dust, wake up and sing. Glad will be the people when he ruleth. The name of the ungodly

will perish. But to his anointed, the Messiah David, he giveth grace. Grant salvation to the eternal people, to David and to his seed forever.

THE FEAST OF DEDICATION: LIGHTS (HANUKKAH)

Since the Feast of Dedication was instituted after the time of the Old Testament, the Torah does not speak of it. The intertestamental apocryphal book of First Maccabees gives us valuable historical insight into the origins of this significant Jewish feast.

Around the year 170 B.C. Antiochus Epiphanes IV ruled Judah in despotic horror. He crushed the Jews, murdered the priests, profaned the altar, and snuffed out the holy lights of the sanctuary. History tells us this monstrous beast of a man required the Jews to profane the Sabbath, feasts, and sanctuary. He demanded that they build altars and shrines for idols, sacrifice swine, and leave their sons uncircumcised. Temple chambers were turned into brothels. Mothers who had their infant sons circumcised were crucified with their children hanging around their necks. Over eighty thousand Jews died, and many others were sold into slavery. These were dark days in Israel.

But in 160 B.C. a Hasmonean priestly family, known as the Maccabees (meaning hammerers), led a successful revolt against Antiochus Epiphanes. In 165 B.C. Judas Maccabaeus restored the desecrated temple on Kislev 25 (November-December). The Jews celebrated in a joyous service of rededication. The Apocrypha records,

Early in the morning on the twenty-fifth day of the ninth month, which is the month of Kislev, in the one

*hundred and forty-eighth year, they rose and offered
sacrifice, as the law directs, on the new altar of burnt
offering that they had built. At the very season and on
the very day that the Gentiles had profaned it, it was
dedicated with songs and harps and lutes and
cymbals. And all the people fell on their faces and
worshiped and blessed Heaven, who had prospered
them. So they celebrated the dedication of the altar for
eight days, and offered burnt offerings with gladness;
they offered a sacrifice of deliverance and praise. They
decorated the front of the temple with golden crowns
and small shields; they restored the gates and the
chambers for the priests, and furnished them with
doors. There was very great gladness among the
people, and the reproach of the Gentiles was removed.
Then Judas and his brothers and all the assembly of
Israel determined that every year at the same season
the days of the dedication of the altar should be
observed with gladness and joy for eight days,
beginning from the twenty-fifth day of the month of
Kislev.*

(1 Maccabees 4:52–59 RSV)

Tradition has it that the temple *menorah* (lamp) burned
for eight days on one day's supply of oil—a miracle.
"When on the twenty-fifth of Kislev the Jews had
emerged victorious over their foes and destroyed them,
they reentered the temple where they found only one jar
of pure oil, enough to be lit for only a single day; yet they
used it for lighting the required set of lamps for eight

days, until they managed to press olives and produce pure oil."* The rededication of the temple and its miracle of lights gave rise to. the name "Feast of Lights."

JESUS AND THE FEAST OF LIGHTS

The Gospel says,

> *And it was at Jerusalem the feast of the dedication, and it was winter. And Jesus walked in the temple in Solomon's porch. Then came the Jews round about him, and said unto him, How long dost thou make us to doubt? If thou be the Christ, tell us plainly. Jesus answered them, I told you, and ye believed not; the works that I do in my Father's name, they bear witness of me. But ye believe not, because ye are not of my sheep, as I said unto you. My sheep hear my voice, and I know them, and they follow me. And I give unto them eternal life; and they shall never perish, neither shall any man pluck them out of my Father's hand. I and my Father are one.*
>
> (John 10:22–30)

In keeping with custom, Messiah visited the temple during the Feast of Dedication to remember the purification of the temple. And while He walked in Solomon's porch, where the rabbis taught their students, the Master Rabbi gave one of His most profound teachings. The rabbis approached Him, demanding that He explicitly say He was Messiah. Christ proceeded to tell the

---

*Moses Maimonides, *Mishneh Torah*, trans. Philip Birnbaum (New York: Hebrew Publishing Co., 1974), p. 110.

rabbis that not only was He the Good Shepherd but He was also the giver of eternal life and He was one with the God of Israel, His Father. This was His messianic claim. But the Jews rejected Him because His claim did not coincide with their concept of who Messiah would be.

Hanukkah **Today**

The Jews remember the contempt Antiochus had for God and the Torah, but they also remember the daring of Judas Maccabaeus and the rekindling of the great temple *menorah*. At Hanukkah, the Feast of Lights, the Jews sing,

> Rock of Ages, let our song
> Praise thy saving power;
> Thou amidst the raging foes
> Wast our sheltering tower.
> Furious they assailed us,
> But thy arm availed us,
> And thy word broke their sword
> When our own strength failed us.
> And thy word broke their sword
> When our own strength failed us.

The Menorah

Today in Israel on the first night of Hanukkah, Israelis light a torch in the ancient city of Modin, which was the home of the Maccabees. Then a runner carries it to scouts positioned at other points, lighting their torches from it. The light is carried by relay throughout Israel. Other large *menorah* are lit in cities, synagogues, and on walls and towers.

The *menorah* used in homes has nine places for candles. The ninth one is the "work candle" or "servant candle" (*shamash*). Each night one candle is lit from the servant candle, until all eight candles are burning on the last night. The father recites the blessing while the candles are lit. "Blessed art Thou, Lord our God, King of the universe, who has sanctified us with His commandments and commanded us to kindle the Hanukkah light. Blessed art Thou, Lord our God, King of the universe, who has performed miracles for our forefathers in those days, at this time." The *menorah* is placed in or near a window to be a public display of the miracle in the temple years ago. The festive spirit is expressed in prayers, songs, stories about the Maccabees, and family togetherness.

The Dreidel

Jewish tradition says that when Antiochus Epiphanes outlawed the study of Torah, the Jews studied it anyway. They kept a top nearby so that when the authorities broke in to arrest them for studying the Torah, they would hide the scroll and pretend to be playing a game with the spinning top (dreidel). Today's dreidels are four-sided tops bearing Hebrew letters which mean "a great miracle happened there." It is a custom to spin the top at Hanukkah celebrations. Some tops are hollow and will hold candy and small coins for the children.

Gifts

Hanukkah is celebrated as a happy holiday, complete with daily gift giving and the sending of Hanukkah cards. The adults give coins (*gelt*) to the children, who go from relative to relative collecting the coins. The bright coins are placed in the dreidels and taped to the gift boxes.

Giving to needy families (*tzedakah*) is also a traditional practice. Some of the coins, gifts, and *latkes* (traditional potato pancakes fried in oil to represent the oil that miraculously burned in the ancient *menorah*) are brought to the poor. At Hanukkah Jewish families also give money to help the poor, to purchase Israel bonds, and to buy trees for Israel.

Hanukkah and Christmas: Feasts of Light

Many similarities can be found in the Jew's celebration of Hanukkah and the Christian's celebration of Christmas:

1. Both are celebrated on the twenty-fifth of the month.

2. Both commemorate a miracle: Hanukkah, the lasting oil; Christmas, the virgin birth of Christ.

3. Both commemorate deliverance and freedom.

4. Both are celebrated with lights.

5. Both are celebrated with gift exchanges.

6. Both are celebrated with song and prayer.

7. Both are celebrated with festive foods.

8. Both are centered in the home as well as the church or synagogue.

9. Both rely on the servant light (Servant Light), the *shamash.*

The prophet Isaiah saw the living light, the servant of Israel and cried:

> *Arise, shine, for thy light is come, and the glory of the LORD is risen upon thee. For, behold, the darkness shall cover the earth, and gross darkness the people: but the LORD shall arise upon thee, and his glory shall be seen upon thee. And the Gentiles shall come to thy light, and the kings to the brightness of thy rising.*
> (Isa. 60:1–3)

Chapter 7

THE TORAH'S LIVING SYMBOL

Scripture for study:

> *And when the dew that lay was gone up, behold, upon the face of the wilderness there lay a small round thing, as small as the hoar frost on the ground. And when the children of Israel saw it, they said one to another, It is manna: for they wist not what it was. And Moses said unto them, This is the bread which the LORD hath given you to eat. This is the thing which the LORD hath commanded, Gather of it every man according to his eating, an omer for every man, according to the number of your person; take ye every man for them which are in his tents. And the children of Israel did so, and gathered, some more, some less. And when they did mete it with an omer, he that gathered little had no lack; they gathered every man according to his eating.*
>
> (Exod. 16:14–18)

> *I am the bread of life. Your fathers did eat manna in*
> *the wilderness, and are dead. This is the bread which*
> *cometh down from heaven, that a man may eat*
> *thereof, and not die. I am the living bread which came*
> *down from heaven: if any man eat of this bread, he*
> *shall live forever: and the bread that I will give is my*
> *flesh, which I will give for the life of the world.*
> (John 6:48–51)

Out of the rich symbolism of the Torah, the Jews drew three types or prefiguring symbols to point to the Messiah. All three symbols came from the wilderness experience of the Israelites. All three symbols were carried into other festivals and customs over the years. From all three types the Jews formed their expectations of what the coming Messiah would be like. And in all three cases Jesus declared Himself to be the fulfillment of those symbols.

BREAD OF LIFE

In the wilderness the Israelites called to God for food, and He supplied a kind of bread they had never seen before: "And when the dew that lay was gone up, behold, upon the face of the wilderness there lay a small round thing, as small as the hoar frost on the ground. . . . And Moses said unto them, This is the bread which the LORD hath given you to eat" (Exod. 16:14–15). They called the unfamiliar food *manna,* meaning "What is it?" According to Exodus 16:31, "The taste of it was like wafers made with honey." Psalm 78:25 described it as "angels' food." J. Orr's studies of manna revealed:

It was light, nutritious, palatable, comprised variety by admitting of being prepared in different ways—baked, seethed, etc. (Exodus 16:23; Numbers 11:8); was abundant in quantity, readily distinguishable by the eye, and being of a granulated nature, and strewn thickly throughout all the camp, could be collected with a very moderate expenditure of labor. It was thus, like so much in our own surroundings, and in the provision which God makes for our wants, a constant witness to the care, goodness, wisdom, and forethought of the great Giver.

God's provision of manna was not a one-time event; He sustained Israel with it for forty years. No natural phenomena could have provided for a million people (a conservative figure) daily for forty years in a barren land. Wild cereal crops or the drippings of desert trees and shrubs could never supply such a demand. Some estimates have indicated that the Israelites needed 1,500,000 pounds of food per week to survive.

In spite of God's miraculous provision, the Israelites failed to obey the Torah's regulations about manna. They attempted to hoard it from one day to the next and encountered disaster (Exod. 16:20). They also tried to gather manna on the Sabbath, in spite of God's warning that none would be given that day (Exod. 16:26–27).

The Israelites did, however, memorialize God's provision by placing a golden pot of manna in the ark of the covenant (Exod. 16:33–34). The pot contained one omer, about two quarts, just enough for one day's need. Seemingly it was preserved, untouched by decay or mold, from the day Moses placed it in the ark until 586 B.C. when the temple was sacked and destroyed. The manna may have been removed earlier by the Philistines (1 Sam. 4:11); it may have been moved by Aaron himself and placed "before the Testimony" (Exod. 16:34); or it may have been moved for the dedication of the temple (1 Kings 8:9).

Over the years the Jews increasingly saw the manna as a symbol of the coming Messiah. According to a legend of the rabbis, Jeremiah the prophet hid away the gold pot of manna in a cave on Mount Sinai when the temple was destroyed by Nebuchadnezzar. They believed that when Messiah came, He would feed the people of God during the messianic kingdom.

The rabbis repeatedly associated bread and abundance with Messiah's coming. They said, "The kernels of wheat will be as big as two bulls' kidneys," and "Wheat stalks will rise higher than palm trees." They taught that such abundant wheat would supply "new manna" in the kingdom age.

When Jesus provided bread for the 5,000 people who followed Him one day, He naturally caught the attention of the Jews who knew the rabbinic predictions. They expected Him to repeat the sign of providing bread in order to fulfill His messianic claim. "They said, therefore, unto him, What sign showest thou, then, that we may see, and believe thee? What does thou work? Our fathers did eat manna in the desert; as it is written, He gave them bread from heaven to eat" (John 6:30–31). Jesus accepted their challenge by claiming that He was not merely the giver but the Living Bread itself: "I am the bread of life; he that cometh to me shall never hunger" (John 6:35b). He went on to chastise the Jews who "murmured at him" because of His claim by saying, "This is the bread which came down from heaven, not as your fathers did eat manna, and are dead; he that eateth of this bread shall live for ever" (John 6:58).

The rabbis believed that their forefathers who died in the desert missed not only the Promised Land but also the life to come through their disobedience. Jesus prodded the Jewish conscience when He pointed out the shortcomings of the manna they sought. It could neither prevent death nor bring spiritual life. Only Jesus, the Bread of Life, could say, "He that eateth of this bread shall live for ever" (John 6:58b).

LIVING WATER

At Meribah the whole company of Israel murmured against Moses as they drank the last drop of water in their water-skins (Exod. 17:2–7). They had been out of Egypt three months. Their last refreshment had come at Elim where they had found twelve springs of water and seventy palm trees. They had not yet made it to Mount Sinai. Scouts brought in word that they faced utter drought ahead. Depressed hearts cried for water, and from the rock at Horeb, God supplied it.

From this early incident at Meribah until arriving at Kadesh thirty-eight years later, the Israelites did not complain for water again. Approximately one and a half million people and their cattle had sufficient water. The need could have been as much as two million gallons per day for thirty-eight years! Israel was constantly refreshed by rivers in the desert (Ps. 105:41). According to rabbinic tradition, the rock of Horeb actually followed the desert wanderers, providing refreshment.

After thirty-eight years a new generation needed to

experience the power of God. Water again became scarce at Kadesh, and the Israelites repeated the complaint of their fathers; God again provided a miracle from the rock (Num. 20:1–11).

From the time of the Exodus, the Jews viewed water as a symbol of life and hope. Their water supply was always scarce, and those who owned it were usually wealthy. The poor, on the other hand, found themselves in danger of dying of thirst. Isaiah highlighted the plight of the poor when he cried, "Ho, every one that thirsteth, come ye to the waters, and he that hath no money; come . . . without money and without price" (Isa. 55:1).

The Jews used the term *living water* for water that flowed from a river or stream. Running water was purer than water from a stagnant pool. Rabbis also spoke of living water in a spiritual sense as the satisfaction of knowing God Himself. They took their symbolism from David's words: "As the hart panteth after the water brooks, so panteth my soul after thee, O God" (Ps. 42:1). The prophet Jeremiah also portrayed God as the source of living water: "For my people have committed two evils: they have forsaken me, the fountain of living waters, and hewed them out cisterns, broken cisterns, that can hold no water" (Jer. 2:13).

Often the rabbis identified living water as wisdom from the Torah or as Torah study itself. Because Israel once suffered greatly by going three days without water (Exod. 15:22), the rabbis made the application that Israel must not allow three days to pass without study of the Torah.

The rabbinic sages also believed that the messianic age would be a time of quenched thirst for the earth and God's people. They took their direction from the prophets:

For with thee is the fountain of life.

(Ps. 36:9a)

And the parched ground shall become a pool, and the thirsty land springs of water.

(Isa. 35:7a)

They shall not hunger nor thirst, neither shall the heat nor sun smite them.

(Isa. 49:10a)

And it shall be, in that day, that living waters shall go out from Jerusalem.

(Zech. 14:8a)

Israel's religious leaders so loved the symbolism of living water that they introduced a Water-Drawing Ceremony into the Feast of Tabernacles. Since the Scripture gave no directives for the ceremony, the exact reasons for it are now unclear. But probably the water offering commemorated God's provision in the wilderness. Also since the Feast of Tabernacles coincided with the need for winter rains, the offering symbolized Israel's petition for rain.

The Water-Drawing Ceremony was a joyous celebration. On the last day of the Feast of Tabernacles (Succoth), a great procession from the temple went to the pool of Siloam. Led by the temple musicians and dancing white-robed priests, they marched through the water gate, down the hill of Zion to the pool. The priests then filled golden vessels with water. When the procession returned to the temple, they emptied the vessels on the altar as the Levites chanted, ". . . with joy shall ye draw water out of the wells of salvation" (Isa. 12:3).

Several New Testament writers portrayed Jesus as the Living Water anticipated by the Jews. Paul alluded to the rabbinic teaching regarding the rock of Horeb in 1 Corinthians 10:1–4: "Moreover, brethren, I would not that ye should be ignorant, how that all our fathers . . . did all drink the same spiritual drink: for they drank of that spiritual Rock that followed them, and that Rock was Christ." According to Paul, Jesus was with Israel all through the wilderness, sustaining them with the water of life.

Jesus also described Himself as the fountain of living water to the Samaritan woman:

> *Jesus answered, and said unto her, If thou knewest the gift of God, and who it is that saith to thee, Give me to drink, thou wouldest have asked of him, and he would have given thee living water. The woman saith unto him, Sir, thou hast nothing to draw with, and the well is deep; from whence, then, hast thou that living water? Art thou greater than our father, Jacob, which gave us the well, and drank thereof himself, and his children, and his cattle? Jesus answered, and said unto her, Whosoever drinketh of this water shall thirst again; But whosoever drinketh of the water that I shall give him shall never thirst, but the water that I shall give him shall be in him a well of water springing up into everlasting life.*
>
> (John 4:10–14)

Jesus' encounter with the Samaritan woman was personal and instructive. He gently drew her from the concept of living, running water to the spiritual picture of the life-giving Spirit of God. But at the Water-Drawing

Ceremony of the Feast of Tabernacles, Jesus' announcement was public and corrective. As He watched the customary spectacle of pouring water on the altar, He stood and interrupted the gaiety of the celebration. He shouted to the huge crowd, "If any man thirst, let him come unto me, and drink. He that believeth on me, as the scripture hath said, out of his belly shall flow rivers of living water" (John 7:37–38).

But Jesus did not enter into the postbiblical practice of the Water-Drawing Ceremony because it was not commanded by the Torah. His abrupt announcement during the ceremony implied a rebuke. Yet He saw in the Water-Drawing Ceremony a figure of His own role in issuing the Holy Spirit, and He declared Himself to be the Water of Life.

LIGHT OF THE WORLD

On Mount Sinai, Moses saw the glory of the Lord, or *Shekhinah*, meaning "the dwelling" of the Lord (Exod. 24:15–17). Throughout the Old Testament we are told that whenever God chose to visit a person or place, the Shekhinah also appeared on that person or place as a sign of His presence. After appearing on Mount Sinai, the Shekhinah filled the tabernacle: "Then a cloud covered the tent of the congregation, and the glory of the LORD filled the tabernacle. And Moses was not able to enter into the tent of the congregation, because the cloud abode thereon, and the glory of the LORD filled the tabernacle" (Exod. 40:34–35). The pillar of fire that led Israel by night also represented the presence of God in blazing light (Exod. 13:21). In every case the Shekhinah was a bright and blinding light—too bright for men and women to look at.

To symbolize the light of Shekhinah, the seven-branched lampstand (*menorah*) illuminated the Holy Place of the tabernacle. As the only light in the Holy Place, it was placed directly outside the veil, in front of the ark (Exod. 27:20–21). Beaten of one solid piece of gold, the lampstand weighed about 108 pounds. It was shaped into seven branches with cups for pure, golden olive oil. The Torah required that the lamps be lit every night (Exod. 27:21; 30:8).

As a symbol for the very presence of God, "light" was a favorite topic for rabbinic discussion. Hebrew sages developed a series of traditions about the idea of the Shekhinah. According to the rabbis, the Shekhinah rested upon all the pious and righteous. The sages taught that the Shekhinah appeared when a *minyan* (quorum of ten Jews) was praying, when two Jews engaged in Torah study, or when one Jew recited the *Shema* (Deut. 6:4–9). The sages said the Shekhinah rested on the house where husband and wife lived in peace, as well as on the benevolent and hospitable. The sages believed that the glory of God appeared to Moses in the burning bush; they expected the same light to illumine the world of the future. The Talmud said that wherever Israel went, the Shekhinah followed. The rabbis believed that when the Jews were in exile, the Shekhinah was also in exile.

The Jews also formed many traditions surrounding the *menorah* or perpetual lamp. While the Torah required lighting the lamp every evening, the rabbis established the custom of lighting only the six branches of the candlestick every evening and keeping the central candle constantly burning. If the central candle went out, the rabbis came to believe that disaster impended. They interpreted the meaning of the *menorah* differently: some said the seven lamps represented the sevenfold perfect vision of the eyes of the Lord; others identified the seven lamps with the seven days of creation; others simply referred to the *menorah* as the Shekhinah itself, the light of God. According to Jewish legend, God hid the *menorah* from Nebuchadnezzar when he sacked and burned the temple. Many rabbis believed that the *menorah*, along with the other five articles of temple furniture, would be restored for a new temple during the messianic kingdom.

Since light was always associated with God in Hebrew thinking, the rabbis frequently associated the concept of light with the Messiah. They declared that Messiah's name would be "Light." They gathered abundant evidence for their idea in the writings of the prophets:

> *The LORD is my light and my salvation.*
>
> (Ps. 27:1a)

> *Arise, shine; for thy light is come, and the glory of the LORD is risen upon thee.*
>
> (Isa. 60:1)

> *The LORD shall be thine everlasting light.*
>
> (Isa. 60:20b)

> *The LORD shall be a light unto me.*
>
> (Mic. 7:8c)

Because of the symbolism of light in Israel's traditions, the Jews established a lighting ceremony at the Feast of Tabernacles. It occurred on the evening of the first day of the feast and was a prelude to the Water-Drawing Ceremony. With a spectacular blaze of light, the ceremony was a memorial to the Shekhinah and the fiery pillar in the wilderness.

The ceremony began in the outer court of the temple, with the pious men of the synagogues and the priests dancing through the night, carrying torches in their hands. The Levites sang praises to God, accompanied by lyres, harps, flutes, and cymbals. Arriving in the Court of Women, the priests lit four golden candlesticks, which were seventy-five feet tall. Tradition says the candlewicks had been made of the worn-out robes of the priests from that year. The lighting of the giant candlesticks signaled the illumination of blazes all over the city and surrounding hills until, as the Talmud said, "There was no courtyard in Jerusalem that was not made brilliant with the light."

Following that spectacular celebration of lights, Jesus declared to the Pharisees, "I am the light of the world; he that followeth me shall not walk in darkness, but shall have the light of life" (John 8:12). He was clearly making a messianic declaration, and the Pharisees recognized His claim (John 8:13).

As Jesus looked at the lights of the city and knew the darkness in the souls of the city's people, He cried out that He was more than a temple light; He was the Light of the entire world. He rebuked the Pharisees for their unbelief, and Paul later explained that action in terms of light; "But all things that are reproved are made manifest by the light: for whatsoever doth make manifest is light" (Eph. 5:13).

Many other New Testament writers pointed to Jesus as the Light. Mark 9:1–7 declares that Jesus was transfigured before Peter, James, and John in His original light. Later, Saul of Tarsus fell prostrate in the dust at the sight of the Shekhinah surrounding Jesus (Acts 9:3–5). On Patmos, John the aged fell down as if he were dead when Jesus appeared to him in the blazing light of seven candlesticks (Rev. 1:12–18).

According to these witnesses, the Light which the rabbis were seeking came in Jesus. As John said of Him, "We beheld his glory" (John 1:14).

Chapter 8

THE TORAH'S GREATEST INTERPRETER

Scripture for study:

> And it shall come to pass in the last days, that the mountain of the LORD'S house shall be established in the top of the mountains, and shall be exalted above the hills; and all nations shall flow unto it. And many people shall go and say, Come ye, and let us go up to the mountain of the LORD, to the house of the God of Jacob; and he will teach us of his ways, and we will walk in his paths; for out of Zion shall go forth the law, and the word of the LORD from Jerusalem.
>
> (Isa. 2:2–3)

> Whosoever, therefore, shall break one of these least commandments, and shall teach men so, he shall be called the least in the kingdom of heaven: but whosoever shall do and teach them, the same shall be called great in the kingdom of heaven. For I say unto you that except your righteousness shall exceed the

*righteousness of the scribes and Pharisees, ye shall in
no case enter into the kingdom of heaven.*

(Matt. 5:19–20)

*And it came to pass, when Jesus had ended these
sayings, the people were astonished at his doctrine; for
he taught them as one having authority, and not as
the scribes.*

(Matt. 7:28–29)

When Jesus preached His great Sermon on the Mount
(Matt. 5:3–7:27), He frequently stated, "Ye have heard
that it was said by them of old time. . . ." His words
carried four possible meanings:

1. He referred to the Written Torah.

2. He referred to the "sayings" from the Written Torah,
   sayings on which the learned Jews relied.

3. He referred to the "sayings" of the ancient Oral
   Torah.

4. He referred to more recent rabbinic teachings.

In any case, He largely agreed with the sayings and
acknowledged them as valid. Jesus consistently rejected
the oral traditions of the Jewish Fathers. However, when
He saw useful truth, Jesus made an appeal to traditions
for further instruction. In fact, He frequently tripped up
the Pharisees in their own interpretation of rabbinic
teaching. Messiah was well versed not only in the Torah
but also in the traditional sayings and maxims of the
Fathers.

In the Sermon on the Mount Jesus reinforced the "sayings of old" and then expanded on them with a new kind of authority. When He said, "But I say unto you," He placed Himself above the authority of Moses and the Fathers. He never annulled the Torah, but He exposed the deeper significance that lay in the mind of God. His teaching moved from the surface to the heart, from the external to the spiritual, from the outward ritual to the soul.

RECONCILIATION

The Torah said,

> *And if any one of the common people sin through ignorance, while he doeth somewhat against any of the commandments of the LORD concerning things which ought not to be done, and be guilty; or if his sin, which he hath sinned, come to his knowledge; then he shall bring his offering, a kid of the goats, a female without blemish, for his sin which he hath sinned.*
>
> (Lev. 4:27–28)

Jesus said,

> *Therefore, if thou bring thy gift to the altar, and there rememberest that thy brother hath ought against thee, Leave there thy gift before the altar, and go thy way; first be reconciled to thy brother, and then come and offer thy gift.*
>
> (Matt. 5:23–24)

The rabbis taught that the Day of Atonement atoned for people's offenses against God but not for their offenses against their neighbors. According to the Torah, sacrifice did not cover sins committed willfully, defiantly, or purposely. It taught that atonement covered only the sins committed in ignorance. Therefore, the offenders who knew they had sinned against their neighbors had to redress the wrong they had done.

When Jesus commented on reconciliation, He merely stressed a principle that the Jews already knew but had forsaken in practice. He declared that reconciliation cannot take place between a person and God until that person is reconciled with his or her neighbor. The gift offered at the altar did not suffice for broken human relationships. Jesus had little patience with the externals of religion. Obedience was better than sacrifice; reconciliation was better than the gift; and forgiveness was better than the goat. The breach between people and God cannot be healed until the breach between enemies is healed.

ADULTERY

The Torah said,

> Thou shalt not commit adultery.
>
> (Exod. 20:14)

Jesus said,

> Ye have heard that it was said by them of old time, Thou shalt not commit adultery; But I say unto you, that whosoever looketh on a woman to lust after her

hath committed adultery with her already in his heart.
(Matt. 5:27–28)

The Torah was clear that not only was the overt act of adultery unlawful but the desire was equally sinful (Deut. 5:21). Covetousness or lust was plainly condemned by Mosaic law (Exod. 20:17).

The rabbis who commented on the Torah recognized the seriousness of the lustful look. They said, "Everyone who looks at a woman lustfully is as though he had been in bed with her." Jewish sayings included: "The eye and the hand are the two brokers of evil"; "The heart and the eye are the two handmaids of sin"; "Woe to him who goes after his eyes for they are adulterous." But the rabbis considerably weakened the concept by teaching that a man's good intentions were considered good deeds, but evil intentions were counted against him only if he committed an overt act.

The rabbis also redefined adultery to redistribute the blame and weaken the law. They restricted their definition to sexual intercourse between a Jewish man and the wife (or the betrothed woman) of another Jew. Therefore, the relationship between any man, whether married or unmarried, and an unmarried woman was not considered adultery and was not subject to the condemnation of the Torah. Consequently Jewish men were considerably freer under rabbinic interpretation, and the stress of the law came to rest upon the woman's guilt.

In His Sermon on the Mount, Jesus enforced the teaching of the Torah but attacked the later interpretations. He stressed the guilt inherent in the lustful look and in so doing condemned the Pharisees' self-justification on the issue. The Pharisees, fanatical for the law, insisted on enforcing the seventh commandment by stoning. Their actions left them vulnerable to condemnation for violating the tenth commandment, for they, too, had been guilty of the "lustful look."

Jesus also taught that the guilt of adultery must be shared equally by the man and woman. He plainly nullified rabbinical law by declaring that:

1. Adultery was committed when a man violated any woman, not just another Jew's betrothed or his wife.

2. Adultery was not limited to sexual intercourse.

3. Evil intentions, even without the act, made a person guilty before God.

4. The Jew, knowing the problem of "the eye," did not control his lust.

DIVORCE

The Torah said,

> When a man hath taken a wife, and married her, and it come to pass that she find no favor in his eyes, because he hath found some uncleanness in her; then let him write her a bill of divorcement, and give it in her hand, and send her out of his house. And when she is departed out of his house, she may go and be another man's wife."
>
> (Deut. 24:1-2)

Jesus said,

It hath been said, Whosoever shall put away his wife, let him give her a writing of divorcement; But I say unto you that whosoever shall put away his wife, saving for the cause of fornication, causeth her to commit adultery; and whosoever shall marry her that is divorced committeth adultery.

(Matt. 5:31–32)

According to the Mosaic law, the initiative for a divorce lay with the husband. If he found "some uncleanness" in his wife, he could send her away. But he must also write her a certificate, clarifying her status and allowing her to remarry.

Traditionally the Jews had a higher regard for marriage than any of the nations surrounding them. Rabbinic teaching said, "Unchastity causes the glory of God to depart," and "Every Jew must surrender his life rather than commit idolatry, murder, or adultery." The Jewish Talmud said, "Over him who divorces the wife of his youth, even the altar of God sheds tears." Rabbi Shammai, who preceded the Pharisees, taught that the only cause for divorce was unfaithfulness. He defined the Torah's words "uncleanness" or "some indecency" to mean only sexual unchastity. His followers said, "Let a wife be as mischievous as the wife of Ahab [Jezebel]; she cannot be divorced except for adultery."

Although rabbinic law said that "a woman may be divorced with or without her will, but a man only with his will," later rabbis did seek to protect the divorced woman. They ordered elaborate precautions to insure the validity of the divorce document, guarding her from a vacillating husband.

While the wife could not divorce her husband, she

could persuade the Jewish court to compel her husband to divorce her for three reasons: if he contracted a disease, if he participated in a repulsive trade, or if he forced her to make pledges against her betterment.

Under Hillel the Elder, the father of Pharisaism, reasons for divorce became increasingly lax. Hillel allowed the husband great latitude in determining "some uncleanness." According to Hillel's followers, a husband could divorce his wife if she spoiled his dinner, if she appeared in public with her head uncovered, if she spoke with men in the street, if she criticized her husband's parents, or if she was a nagging wife. Rabbi Akiba said, "If any man saw a woman more beautiful than his own wife, he might put his wife away; because it is said in the Torah, 'if she find not favor in his eyes' (Deut. 24:1)."

Against the Pharisees' legalized divorce at caprice, Jesus clearly and correctly interpreted Moses. He turned back to the original meaning of "some uncleanness" or "some indecency" from Deuteronomy 24:1, defining it simply as unchastity. Later He reiterated His position and explained why the Law had allowed divorce in the first place:

> They say unto him, Why did Moses then command to give a writing of divorcement, and to put her away? He saith unto them, Moses, because of the hardness of your hearts, suffered you to put away your wives, but from the beginning it was not so. And I say unto you, Whosoever shall put away his wife, except it be for fornication, and shall marry another, committeth adultery; and whoso marrieth her which is put away doth commit adultery.
>
> (Matt. 19:7–9)

Whereas under Jewish law the husband had the advantage, Jesus emphasized the man's sin in divorce. By freeing his wife from marriage, the husband exposed her to the temptation of remarriage, and he led the second husband to adultery. The second husband also carried the guilt for knowingly marrying a woman divorced on grounds other than fornication.

On the subject of divorce, Jesus again interpreted the Torah from its earlier meaning and set aside rabbinic additions.

Jewish Divorcement: Then and Now

The Jewish divorce is called a "get." To acquire a "get," Jews follow this process:

1. The party contacts a rabbi.

2. They are directed to the *bet din*, a rabbinical court.

3. The bill of divorcement must be written by hand in Aramaic.

4. A trained scribe is acquired to prepare the document.

5. The document is prepared according to rabbinic ritual and tradition, using special heavy paper, ink that cannot be erased, and a special pen (usually a goose quill).

6. The bill must consist of twelve lines, the number equivalent to the word "get."

7. It must be witnessed by two adult males.

8. Names and places must be spelled correctly. Any misspelling invalidates the document.

9. The rabbi questions the parties.

10. The wife removes her ring.

11. The document is handed to the rabbi, the rabbi hands it to the husband, the husband drops it into the wife's palm and says, "this be your 'get' and with it be you divorced from this time forth, so that you may become the wife of any man."

12. The scribe puts his distinguishing mark on the document.

13. The four corners are cut off so that it cannot be fraudulently used again.

When the husband, in keeping with the traditional Jewish ritual says, ". . . you may become the wife of any man" and divorces his wife for any cause, he makes her an adulteress.

ALMSGIVING

The Torah said,

> *If there be among you a poor man of one of thy brethren within any of thy gates in thy land which the LORD thy God giveth thee, thou shalt not harden thine heart, nor shut thine hand from thy poor brother; But*

thou shalt open thine hand wide unto him, and shalt
surely lend him sufficient for his need, in that which
he wanteth.

(Deut. 15:7–8)

Jesus said,

Take heed that ye do not your alms before men, to be
seen of them; otherwise ye have no reward of your
Father, which is in heaven. Therefore, when thou
doest thine alms, do not sound a trumpet before thee,
as the hypocrites do in the synagogues and in the
streets, that they may have glory of men. Verily I say
unto you, They have their reward. But when thou
doest alms, let not thy left hand know what thy right
hand doeth, That thine alms may be in secret; and thy
Father, which seeth in secret, himself shall reward
thee openly.

(Matt. 6:1–4)

Jewish law required the Israelites to give generously to
the poor. According to the Torah, they left the corners of
their fields unharvested for the poor (Lev. 19:9–10). The
Israelites supplied clothing, furniture, an animal to ride,
and even a wife if necessary, to the poor man. The Torah
commanded that the stranger (Gentile) be treated the
same as the Jew. If a Hebrew encountered a beggar, the
Jew must give something, even a dried fig, because the
Torah forbade sending the poor away "emptyhanded"
(Deut. 15:7; Ps. 74:21). If the poor refused charity, then
the faithful Jew must make the person a loan. Collections
for the needy were gathered weekly so that the poor
could be sustained for seven days at a time.

The Jewish sages considered a gift to the poor meritorious for righteousness. They believed that acts of charity (*tzedakah*) brought redemption nearer and saved the soul from the fires of hell (Gehinnom). Rabbi Joshua ben Korha said, "He who turns his eyes away [from the poor] is to be considered as a worshipper of idols." The Talmud said, "Alms rescues from death and it will cleanse from all sin," and "Greater is he who gives alms than he who offers all sacrifices."

The law about giving to the poor became a field of study on its own. Consequently the minute legal restrictions about giving were abundant.

The Torah required farmers to leave the corners of their fields unharvested for the poor, but the Torah did not indicate the size of the corner to be left. The rabbis decreed that not less than one-sixtieth of the harvest could be considered a corner. If it was a very small field and one-sixtieth of the harvest was too small for any good, then the owner had to increase the allotment to the poor.

Traditionally the Jewish community's synagogues and schools collected the alms for the poor. Rabbis often sounded trumpets for religious occasions requiring alms-giving, especially for periods of fasting. They collected the alms in "boxes of righteousness" shaped like trumpets (and referred to as trumpets in the Talmud).

In spite of the public nature of giving on special occasions, the rabbis warned against ostentation:

1. Whoever gives alms in secret is better than Moses.

2. The giving that saves from death is when the poor person does not know from whom it comes, and when the giver does not know who received it.

3. It is best to drop money when one walks by the poor and not to know who picks it up.

4. It is best to give nothing to the poor than to make them feel ashamed.

5. The best way to give charity is to deposit the money in the collection box. In this manner, the giver does not know the receiver, and the poor does not know the giver.

6. A benefaction to the poor must be given privately, with no one else near.

7. Far better if you give nothing to the poor than that the whole world should watch you hand out charity. For you have humiliated the poor with it.

The Pharisees set aside the nobler teachings of the rabbis in their practice of giving. They learned to fling their coins into the trumpet collection places hard enough to make a ringing sound, calling public attention to their benevolence. Probably certain rich men publicly designated a certain day on which to distribute their alms.

Messiah heartily sanctioned almsgiving, but He opposed ostentation. Giving was to be practiced with the purest motives. The Christian reader may not detect it, but Jesus touched on the three great pillars of Jewish piety—almsgiving, prayer, and fasting—in His Sermon on the Mount.

Jesus censured the hypocrisy of the Pharisees whose practice in giving contradicted even their own teaching. He portrayed a Pharisee finding a conspicuous place in the city, sounding his trumpet, gathering around him the poor and handicapped, and showering gifts upon them.

Jesus returned to the idea of secrecy in charity. In giving alms, He found expression for character. He stressed that the truly pious shall keep their giving secret from other people—even from themselves as much as possible. He suggested that one should give alms for the sake of the heavenly Father.

Jewish Almsgiving: Then and Now

Rabbis believed that when God gave wealth to the rich, He gave it in trust to the poor. Since the Torah commanded Jews to also love the stranger, the Gentile poor as well as the Jewish poor gleaned at the harvest. Gentiles were to be clothed, fed, and given shelter. The Gentile sick were to be cared for, and their dead were to be given decent burial.

The rules for almsgiving included the following:

1. One must feed and clothe the poor of the nations together with the poor of Israel.

2. Each person was required to give to the poor according to personal means. Even a poor person who received charity must also give a little to charity.

3. The amount of charity is a tenth after taxes.

4. One must care for the poor in one's household (mother and father) before the poor in one's city. The poor in Israel took precedence over the poor in other nations.

5. It was forbidden to rebuke or raise one's voice in anger at a poor person, for that person's spirit was already broken.

6. The scholar engaged in biblical studies was to be given an income, relieving him of worry for a livelihood. Rabbinical law, however, stressed the virtue of honest labor, even for a scholar.

7. It was virtuous to encourage others to give to charity.

8. The pledge must be paid immediately.

9. One should work for independence and not resort to public assistance. Even menial work is a virtue.

10. One must not be too proud to accept charity.

11. Lending to the poor was more virtuous than giving charity to a beggar.

12. One cannot press for the return of a loan if it was known the repayment was not yet available.

13. One cannot procrastinate to repay if the repayment is available.

The Yom Kippur service emphasizes that repentance, prayer, and charity avert the harshness of God's judgment. Jews give to charity on the eve of Yom Kippur, believing that the act of giving alms pardons from transgressions. Because charity is considered effective in the redemption of both the living and the dead, offerings for charity are also received at funerals.

Maimonides taught eight ways to give charity, each way better than the former:

1. To give grudgingly.

2. To give less than one should, but to give cheerfully.

3. To give directly to the poor when asked.

4. To give directly to the poor before being asked.

5. To give indirectly so that the donor does not know the recipient.

6. To give so that the recipient does not know the donor.

7. To give so that both donor and recipient do not know each other.

8. The highest form of charity is to give the help before a person becomes poor. The aid may come through a loan, employment, or some sort of rehabilitation, which allows the person to retain self-respect.

Paul gives us the perfect example of charity. "For ye know the grace of our Lord Jesus Christ, that, though he was rich, yet for your sakes he became poor, that ye through his poverty might be rich" (2 Cor. 8:9).

PRAYER

The Torah said,

> And the LORD appeared to Solomon by night, and said
> unto him, I have heard thy prayer, and have chosen
> this place to myself for a house of sacrifice. If I shut up
> heaven that there be no rain, or if I command the
> locusts to devour the land, or if I send pestilence
> among my people; If my people, which are called by
> my name, shall humble themselves, and pray, and
> seek my face, and turn from their wicked ways, then
> will I hear from heaven, and will forgive their sin,
> and will heal their land. Now mine eyes shall be open,
> and mine ears attent unto the prayer that is made in
> this place. For now have I chosen and sanctified this
> house, that my name be there for ever, and mine eyes
> and mine heart shall be there perpetually.
>
> (2 Chron. 7:12–16)

Jesus said,

> And when thou prayest, thou shalt not be as the
> hypocrites are; for they love to pray standing in the
> synagogues and in the corners of the streets, that they
> may be seen of men. Verily I say unto you, They have
> their reward. But thou, when thou prayest, enter into
> thy closet, and when thou hast shut thy door, pray to
> thy Father, which is in secret; and thy Father, which
> seeth in secret, shall reward thee openly. But when ye
> pray, use not vain repetitions, as the heathen do; for
> they think that they shall be heard for their much
> speaking. Be not ye, therefore, like unto them; for

> *your Father knoweth what things ye have need of,*
> *before ye ask him.*
>
> (Matt. 6:5–8)

Neither the Torah nor the prophets left room for insincere prayer. God's prayer directions to Solomon were precise, with no room for hypocrisy in the words, "If my people, which are called by my name, shall humble themselves, and pray. . . ." God would bring forgiveness and healing to the nation only on the condition of humility and penitent prayer.

Jewish law prescribed that Jews—wherever they happened to be at the time—were required to pray at specific times of the day: 9:00 in the morning, 12:00 noon, and 3:00 in the afternoon. The full *Shema* also had to be recited twice a day, once before 9:00 in the morning and once before 9:00 in the evening. Again, this prayer requirement was binding wherever the Jews found themselves. Upon these regulations a pious Jew daily repeated the Eighteen Benedictions. Although the intention of these requirements was to provide the Jews with a frequent channel of communication with God, the reality was that the prayers became habitual formality, superstitious incantations.

Jewish literature says that a Jew should recite at least one hundred blessings a day. Prayer covered every conceivable area of life, from the hearing of thunder to the leaving of the toilet.

The great rabbis commented extensively on prayer:

1. Great is prayer, greater than all good works.

2. Whoever prays within one's house surrounds it with a wall that is stronger than iron.

3. If a person prays, as if to get through a set task, that is no prayer.

4. God says to Israel, pray in the synagogue of your city; if you cannot, pray in the field; if you cannot, pray in your house; if you cannot, pray on your bed; if you cannot, commune with your own heart upon your bed, and be still.

5. It is forbidden to lengthen out the praise of the Holy One for it says in the Psalms, "Who can utter the mighty doings of the Lord, or show forth all his praise."

6. A person in whom is hypocrisy brings wrath upon the world, and that person's prayer is not heard.

7. While other nations rely on the might of their arms, Israel's weapon is prayer.

8. A new prayer should be said every day.

9. If the mind does not know what the lips are saying, prayer is not prayer.

10. Whoever prays with the assembly shall have that prayer answered.

Other regulations governing prayer included the belief that prayer offered at the temple or synagogue was more efficacious than prayer offered anywhere else. The rabbis believed in long prayers. As one rabbi said, "Whoever is long at prayer is heard."

In His Sermon on the Mount, Jesus pointed out the flaws in the Pharisees' practice of prayer. He did not say that standing to pray in the synagogue was wrong, but standing to be noticed by others was another matter. He censured those people who stood apart in the synagogue, appearing to be absorbed in prayer while secretly hoping to impress others with their piety. According to Jesus, the hypocrites also loved to pray at the appointed hours on street corners, where the population was heavy. This was an obvious case of ostentation. Jesus taught that such prayer accomplished only its purpose of fascinating others; it did not reach the ear of God.

Jesus did not criticize the custom of praying three times a day. But He did point out that the practice could lead to habitual formality. For many Pharisees, the required prayers became nothing more than superstitious incantations.

Messiah taught that if long prayers encouraged vain repetition, then prayer was to be brief and simple. Repetition supposed inattention and ignorance on God's part. Furthermore, real prayer was the language of the heart. Jesus Himself repeated the same prayerful words three times in the Garden of Gethsemane, but His words were not thoughtless repetition.

As the test of sincerity, Jesus asked His followers to pray in secret. Whether the secret chamber He referred to was physical or mental, Jesus suggested that prayers acceptable to God were those that escaped the observation of all other people. He portrayed communication with God as something natural, simple, and easy—that of a child talking with a loving father.

Jewish Prayer: Then and Now

Jewish tradition tells us that in approximately 444 B.C., Ezra and the Sanhedrin instituted the Eighteen Benedictions of prayer, which formed a central weekday prayer called the *amidah*. This prayer, which contained three benedictions of praise, twelve benedictions of various petitions, and three benedictions of thanksgiving, was recited three times daily: 9:00 in the morning, 12:00 noon, and 3:00 in the afternoon. Jews recite the *amidah* while they stand facing the temple in Jerusalem. They cannot pray while standing before anything that would distract them, such as a picture, a statue, or a mirror.

The three specific times of prayer coincided with the times daily sacrifices were offered in the Jerusalem temple. In fact, the rabbis decreed that since the sacrificial system ceased when the temple was destroyed in A.D. 70, prayer was to take the place of animal sacrifices. Prayer was considered to be the sacrifice of the lips to God.

Another way the Jews justified the three daily prayer times was to dedicate them to each of the patriarchs. The morning service was in memory of Abraham, the afternoon service in memory of Isaac, and the evening service in memory of Jacob.

The Jewish posture for prayer has been varied. Whereas Jews always recited the Eighteen Benedictions while they stood, they also offered prayers while they sat. Babylonian influence led the Jews to kneel during worship. The Talmud says that Jews would kneel, prostrate themselves, and kiss the temple floor in Jerusalem. Before the Christian era, Jews would also pray with their hands folded, but when this practice was adopted by the early Christian Jews, the Jews ceased the habit.

Jews have composed extensive lists of blessings to cover almost every area of life. Blessings are to be said for life experiences such as

1. Obtaining new cookware.

2. Beholding a Hebrew graveyard.

3. Listening to thunder.

4. Beholding different-looking people.

5. Beholding over a half-million Jews in one place.

6. Putting on new garments.

7. Standing at the place where miracles had been performed.

8. Reaching the age of seventy.

9. Beholding a house of worship built upon ruins.

10. Finishing a parapet around property for safety.

The rabbis also taught that prayers offered in Hebrew were more virtuous than those said in the vernacular. When the holy name of God was used in prayer, Jews were required to cover their heads. Women were exempt from the set rituals of prayer.

The traditional Jewish prayer book, called the *Siddur* (meaning "arrangement"), has been compiled by hundreds of persons throughout the generations. In it are expressions of Jewish faith, values, sentiments, and experiences. The Mishnah teaches that some of the rabbis meditated for as much as an hour before saying one of the prayers; then the prayer was followed by another two hours of pondering its meaning.

FASTING

The Torah said,

> Also on the tenth day of this seventh month there shall be a day of atonement: it shall be an holy convocation unto you; and ye shall afflict your souls, and offer an offering made by fire unto the LORD. And ye shall do no work in that same day; for it is a day of atonement, to make an atonement for you before the LORD your God. For whatsoever soul it be that shall not be afflicted in that same day, he shall be cut off from among his people.
>
> (Lev. 23:27–29)

Jesus said,

> Moreover, when ye fast, be not, as the hypocrites, of a sad countenance; for they disfigure their faces, that they may appear unto men to fast. Verily I say unto you, They have their reward. But thou, when thou fastest, anoint thine head, and wash thy face, That thou appear not unto men to fast, but unto thy Father, which is in secret; and thy Father, which seeth in secret, shall reward thee openly.
>
> (Matt. 6:16–18)

According to the Torah, all Israelites were to "afflict" or humble themselves by fasting on the Day of Atonement. The Day was spent in solemn self-discipline, denying all pleasure, concentrating on penitence and introspection.

Although the Torah commanded only one official day of fasting, Jewish traditions gradually added others. Many rabbis proclaimed community fast days for special emergencies.

Besides observing national, required fasts, the Pharisees sought additional piety by keeping two fasts each week. Since they believed that Moses ascended and descended from Mount Sinai on Monday and Thursday, they chose those days as weekly fast days. During their fasts, many Pharisees did not comb their hair, wash their faces, or wear shoes. Instead they whitened their faces and put ashes on their heads. They appeared with drawn expressions, considered appropriate for those who were fasting. Since their fast days coincided with market days in Israel, the Pharisees conveniently had a large ready-made audience to behold their piety.

Jesus did not condemn fasting in His sermon. He Himself fasted (Matt. 4:2). He also assumed His disciples would fast at times. But nowhere in the Gospels did the Messiah enjoin His followers to fast out of compulsion or religious duty. He left fasting to individual freedom. In Hebrew culture and from the Torah's teaching, fasting was an expression of humiliation and mourning (2 Sam. 12:16; Isa. 58:3–6; Jonah 3:5). To fast for praise and glory from other people was grand hypocrisy in Jesus' eyes.

He warned His followers to practice their fasts in secret. His disciples were to anoint their heads and wash their faces as signs of joy.

Jewish Fasting: Then and Now

Jewish piety set forth three main objectives for fasting: repentance, supplication for the Lord's help, and mourning with remembrance. The Talmud enjoins fasting as an opportunity to give to charity. Rabbinic sages taught that the true merit of the fast was in the benevolence one gave on the day.

Rabbis developed other fasts throughout Jewish history. They established the Fast of the First-Born on the eve of Passover. They required fasting by the bride and groom on their wedding day. The rabbis eventually added five yearly fasts: one to commemorate the destruction of the first and second temples; one to commemorate Esther's fast before Jewish deliverance in Persia; one to commemorate Gedaliah, a governor of Judah; one to commemorate the Babylonian siege of Jerusalem; and one to commemorate a number of calamities in Israel.

Fasts on Yom Kippur and on the day commemorating the destruction of the temple are total fasts. All eating and drinking is forbidden from before sundown until nightfall of the next day. Strict rules for the fast that commemorates the destruction of the temple require that:

1. Jews may not study the Torah because it gladdens the heart.

2. Jews may not work until the afternoon of the fast day.

3. Jews must sit on low stools until the afternoon of the fast day.

4. Jews may not wear leather shoes.

5. Jewish males may not shave and women may not wear makeup.

6. Jews may not bathe for comfort.

7. Jews may not have sexual intercourse.

8. Jews may not marry during a fast.

9. Jews may not have parties.

10. Jews may not listen to inspiring music.

OATHS

The Torah said,

> *Thou shalt not take the name of the LORD thy God in vain; for the LORD will not hold him guiltless that taketh his name in vain.*

> (Exod. 20:7)

Jesus said,

> *Again, ye have heard that it hath been said by them of old time, Thou shalt not forswear thyself, but shalt perform unto the Lord thine oaths; But I say unto you, Swear not at all; neither by heaven, for it is God's throne; Nor by the earth, for it is his footstool; neither by Jerusalem, for it is the city of the great King. Neither shalt thou swear by thy head, because thou canst not make one hair white or black. But let*

> *your communication be, Yea, yea; Nay, nay: for*
> *whatsoever is more than these cometh of evil.*
>
> (Matt. 5:33–37)

The Torah forbade all perjury or violation of oaths and vows. In ancient Israel the Jews were allowed to swear by the name of God (Deut. 10:20), but such an oath carried an attached curse (Deut. 23:21–23). If people swore by God's name falsely, they invited divine punishment. A typical oath like, "may God's harm come to me and more if . . ." contained the self-curse in the statement.

By the time of Jesus, rabbinic law had substantially changed the customs about oaths. The rabbis had divided oaths into two categories: those that were binding and those that were not. Any oath that bore the name of God was absolutely binding. But any oath sworn by heaven, earth, Jerusalem, or the head was not binding and could be evaded.

Jesus taught that all oaths ultimately appealed to God. He did not comment on the proper use of oaths in the Torah, but He prohibited the rash, idle swearing that had become common among the Jews. He reserved the oath for proper, solemn occasions and not for idle swearing. He censured the evasive wording of oaths (by heaven, earth, Jerusalem, the head), which hid truth with equivocation or reservation. Jesus taught the simple necessity of telling the truth without the need for an oath. He expected His disciples to be committed to truth in Him, preventing the need for any swearing at all.

Messiah's point is that ideally a person should never need an oath to support or guarantee the truth. For an honest person the simple "yes" and "no" is enough.

Jewish Oaths: Then and Now

Jewish history says that when Jews were put under oath in non-Jewish courts, they suffered great humiliation. During the Middle Ages they were made to wear a wreath of thorns while taking an oath, as a humiliating gesture that they belonged to the people who crucified the Messiah. Jews were also made to stand ankle-deep in water because they had rejected "Christian" baptism. In Saxony, Jews were made to stand on the skin of a sow, a forbidden animal to a pious Jew, while taking an oath.

According to the Torah, three types of oaths were allowed:

1. The adjuration to gain information or to give testimony (Lev. 5:1).

2. The exculpatory oath of a defendant when no witness was available (Exod. 22:10–11).

3. The voluntary vow which bound the taker to do or not to do something (Lev. 5:4).

The Torah also recorded acceptable gestures for oaths. Abraham raised his hand to heaven when he swore that he would take no goods from the king of Sodom (Gen. 14:22–23). Elsewhere oaths were taken by placing one's hand under the thigh of the one being sworn to. Abraham ordered his eldest servant to swear to him in that manner when sending him to find a wife for Isaac (Gen. 24:2–4).

The Jewish Talmud gives some guidelines for the use of oaths:

1. Oaths are relevant only to civil and not to criminal cases (criminals would probably lie under oath anyway).

2. Oaths are admitted only when there is no sufficient evidence.

3. Oaths are not given to known liars, gamblers, etc., or to persons who have once perjured themselves.

4. Oaths are not given to children, to insane persons, or to those who are deaf and dumb.

5. Oaths are given by having the person place a scroll of the Torah on his or her arm and swear by the name of God or by His attributes (Mishnah period).

6. Oaths are given while standing up (Mishnah period).

7. Oaths are given while another person holds the Torah and without the use of God's name. The oath would be administered by another person, and the deponent would simply say "amen" (post-Mishnah period).

8. Oaths at one time had to be given in Hebrew, but later the law allowed the use of the vernacular so that the person could clearly understand the oath.

9. Oaths are taken with a warning of the seriousness of a false oath and divine wrath.

10. Oaths are given with equal warning to the one pressing the case, in order to avoid the unnecessary administration of a solemn oath.

Messiah taught that if each person reverenced the name of God and respected the truth, all oaths and all swearing would be unnecessary. If a person habitually lives in the fear of the Lord, his or her word will be as good as an oath: that person will always speak the truth and will avoid using the name of the Lord in vain. Though the use of oaths may be practiced by courts of law, they have no place in the kingdom of the Messiah. Where there is truth in the soul, the simple, "Yea, yea" or "Nay, nay" is enough (see Matt. 5:37).

Chapter 9

THE TORAH'S MESSIAH

Scripture for study:

> Now the LORD said unto Abram, Get thee out of thy
> country, and from thy kindred, and from thy father's
> house unto a land that I will show thee, And I will
> make of thee a great nation, and I will bless thee, and
> make thy name great; and thou shalt be a blessing.
> And I will bless them that bless thee, and curse him
> that curseth thee: and in thee shall all families of the
> earth be blessed.
>
> (Gen. 12:1–3)

> The scepter shall not depart from Judah, nor a
> lawgiver from between his feet, until Shiloh come; and
> unto him shall the gathering of the people be.
>
> (Gen. 49:10)

> There shall come a Star out of Jacob, and a Scepter
> shall rise out of Israel, and shall smite the corners of

Moab, and destroy all the children of Sheth. . . . Out of Jacob shall come he that shall have dominion, and shall destroy him that remaineth of the city.

(Num. 24:17, 19)

Brothers, let me take an example from everyday life. Just as no one can set aside or add to a human covenant that has been duly established, so it is in this case. The promises were spoken to Abraham and to his seed. The Scripture does not say "and to seeds," meaning many people, but "and to your seed," meaning one person, who is Christ. What I mean is this: The law, introduced 430 years later, does not set aside the covenant previously established by God and thus do away with the promise. For if the inheritance depends on the law, then it no longer depends on a promise; but God in his grace gave it to Abraham through a promise. What, then, was the purpose of the law? It was added because of transgressions until the Seed to whom the promise referred had come. The law was put into effect through angels by a mediator.

(Gal 3:15–19 NIV)

The Torah's preeminent purpose was the unfolding of God's redemptive plan not only for Israel but also for the whole human race. Throughout its sacred scrolls of law, history, poetry, and prophecy, a continual foreshadowing pointed to one supreme event—the coming of Messiah as Savior and Lord. As part of His progressive revelation, God chose Israel as the messianic nation, but His redemptive plan was not restricted to Israel alone. From the beginning the Torah pointed to a universal blessing. Fulfillment of that blessing came in the birth, life, ministry, death, resurrection, and exaltation of Jesus, the Messiah.

The new covenant (New Testament) is an outgrowth of the old covenant (Old Testament) and is the authentic and divinely inspired account of God's fulfilled promises. The new covenant does not unfold a new religion or even a new Jewish sect. To the contrary, the new covenant is a continuation of God's revelation and ongoing work among His people.

Thus, the Torah was written to pave the way for Messiah. It is the account of the history of the Israelite nation, coupled with powerful prophecies that pointed to the coming Messiah, King, Priest, and Servant who will rule and bless the entire world. The prophecy and foreshadowing of His appearance constitute the messianic strain in the Torah, forming a scarlet thread that pervades and unifies the many books, chapters, and verses of Scripture. As the prophecies mount, they are accompanied by symbols, pictures, and types, which when taken together could not refer to any other person but Jesus of Nazareth, the prefigured Messiah.

DEFINITION OF MESSIAH

The term *Messiah* comes from the Hebrew *Mashiah*, (rendered *Meshiha* in Aramaic and *Christos* in the Greek Septuagint) meaning to "smear" or to "anoint." Thus Messiah meant the "Anointed One."

In the Torah the term was used to describe kings and priests who were consecrated to their offices by the ceremony of oil anointing. Possibly the later coronation of kings resulted from the ancient rite of oil anointing.

The term *Messiah* as a title was never used in the Torah

as prophetic of a future unique king, with the exception of the phrase "Messiah the Prince" in Daniel 9:25. The term was adopted during the intertestamental period as descriptive of the coming deliverer, the Lord's Anointed, the king of David's line. The term was popularly used when Jesus appeared (John 1:41; 4:25). Jews use the term similarly today.

Israel's concept of Messiah gave the Jews hope in a personal Savior. Unlike all other nations, the Jews lived for the future. Because of the coming Messiah, they clung to their hope in the midst of disaster and defeat; they believed that present despair would eventually result in peace and happiness. Their messianic hope was twofold: first, they looked forward to a glorious state for the nation in the future; second, they hoped for the deliverer who would establish that future kingdom.

MESSIAH AS KING

The Jews' concept of Messiah focused on the idea of the king. Through the nation's powerful king, God could most readily bring about His redemptive purposes. The Israelites believed that the Spirit of God would qualify and anoint the new king with unique power to conquer his enemies and usher in an era of tranquility. They based their ideas primarily on the prophet Nathan's prophecy to David:

> *And when thy days be fulfilled, and thou shalt sleep with thy fathers, I will set up thy seed after thee, which shall proceed out of thy bowels, and I will establish his kingdom. He shall build a house for my name, and I will establish the throne of his kingdom*

> *for ever. I will be his father, and he shall be my son. If*
> *he commit iniquity, I will chasten him with the rod of*
> *men, and with the stripes of the children of men; but*
> *my mercy shall not depart away from him, as I took it*
> *from Saul, whom I put away before thee. And thine*
> *house and thy kingdom shall be established for ever*
> *before thee; thy throne shall be established for ever.*
> (2 Sam. 7:12–16)

David's last words underlined the perpetuity of his house:

> *The Spirit of the* LORD *spake by me, and his word was*
> *in my tongue. The God of Israel said, the Rock of*
> *Israel spake to me, He that ruleth over men must be*
> *just, ruling in the fear of God. And he shall be as the*
> *light of the morning, when the sun riseth, even a*
> *morning without clouds, as the tender grass spring-*
> *ing out of the earth by clear shining after rain.*
> *Although my house be not so with God, yet he hath*
> *made with me an everlasting covenant, ordered in all*
> *things, and sure: for this is all my salvation, and all*
> *my desire, although he make it not to grow.*
> (2 Sam. 23:2–5)

The prophets expanded the idea of a future king. The prophet Isaiah spoke of an extraordinary king in the future, identifying him as "a rod out of the stem of Jesse" or a "root of Jesse" (Isa. 11:1–5, 10–12). Jeremiah called the Messiah the "righteous Branch" (Jer. 23:5–6). Ezekiel alluded to God's "servant David," who would be "prince" and "king" perpetually over the regathered people (Ezek. 34:23–24; 37:24–25). Hosea viewed the reunion of the two kingdoms of Israel and Judah under David's heir (Hos. 3:4–5). Amos also prophesied of the time when the shattered fortunes of Judah would be restored (Amos 9:11–15). Micah described the humble origin of the messianic king: "But thou, Bethlehem Ephratah, though thou be little among the thousands of Judah, yet out of thee shall he come forth unto me that is to be ruler in Israel, whose goings forth have been from of old, from everlasting" (Mic. 5:2).

Thus the Torah clearly and progressively developed the picture of Messiah as a royal son of David and a future, mighty king.

MESSIAH AS PRIEST

The kingship and priesthood were always considered separate offices in ancient Israel, but the prophet Jeremiah alluded to a coming king who would also be a priest: "For thus saith the LORD, David shall never want a man to sit upon the throne of the house of Israel; Neither shall the priests, the Levites, want a man before me to offer burnt offerings, and to kindle meat offerings, and to do sacrifice continually" (Jer. 33:17–18). Jeremiah prophesied that the "new David" would possess priestly rights. Yet the kingship and Levitical priesthood were assured perpetuity based on the covenant with David (Jer. 33:20–22). Jeremiah pointed to a unique kind of king-priest who would not duplicate the Levitical service.

After the Babylonian captivity and reconstruction of Jerusalem, Joshua the high priest assumed prominence in Israel and represented another combination of priest and king. Zechariah portrayed Joshua the priest as being crowned king, symbolizing the union of the kingly and priestly offices in the Messiah:

> *Then take silver and gold, and make crowns, and set them upon the head of Joshua, the son of Josedech, the high priest; And speak unto him, saying, Thus speaketh the LORD of hosts, saying, Behold the man whose name is THE BRANCH; and he shall grow up out of his place, and he shall build the temple of the LORD; Even he shall build the temple of the LORD; and he shall bear the glory, and shall sit and rule upon his throne; and he shall be a priest upon his throne; and the counsel of peace shall be between them both.*
>
> (Zech. 6:11–13)

Psalm 110:1–4 also pictured a united priest and king.

MESSIAH AS A SERVANT

Isaiah introduced the new concept of Messiah as a suffering servant:

> *He is despised and rejected of men, a man of sorrows, and acquainted with grief, and we hid as it were our faces from him; he was despised, and we esteemed him not. Surely he hath borne our griefs, and carried our sorrows; yet we did esteem him stricken, smitten of God, and afflicted. But he was wounded for our transgressions, he was bruised for our iniquities; the chastisement of our peace was upon him, and with his stripes we are healed. All we like sheep have gone astray; we have turned every one to his own way, and the LORD hath laid on him the iniquity of us all. He was oppressed, and he was afflicted, yet he opened not his mouth; he is brought as a lamb to the slaughter, and as a sheep before her shearers is dumb, so he*

openeth not his mouth.

(Isa. 53:3–7)

In this messianic portrait Isaiah described the servant of God offering Himself as a sin offering for the people. Isaiah also predicted that Messiah would be raised from the dead and receive God's riches (Isa. 53:9, 11–12; Ps. 16:10–11). Isaiah portrayed the Messiah communicating His knowledge of salvation to others, making many righteous, and receiving for His suffering the highest of royal splendor:

> *Thus saith the LORD, the Redeemer of Israel, and his Holy One, to him whom man despiseth, to him whom the nation abhorreth, to a servant of rulers: Kings shall see and arise, princes also shall worship, because of the LORD that is faithful, and the Holy One of Israel, and he shall choose thee.*
>
> (Isa. 49:7)

> *So shall he sprinkle many nations; the kings shall shut their mouths at him; for that which had not been told them shall they see, and that which they had not heard shall they consider.*
>
> (Isa. 52:15)

APOCALYPTIC MESSIAH

In the Book of Daniel the apocalyptic idea of the Messiah appeared vividly in another kind of portrayal. According to Daniel, Messiah was seen not as a descendant of David but as a human with superhuman power by whom the Lord established His sovereignty in the earth:

> *I saw in the night visions, and, behold, one like the*
> *Son of man came with the clouds of heaven, and came*
> *to the Ancient of days, and they brought him near*
> *before him. And there was given him dominion and*
> *glory, and a kingdom, that all people, nations, and*
> *languages, should serve him; his dominion is an*
> *everlasting dominion, which shall not pass away, and*
> *his kingdom that which shall not be destroyed.*
> (Dan. 7:13–14)

The Torah described a synthesis of the coming Messiah's characteristics. The Anointed One was destined to be king, priest, servant, and supernatural son of man.

MESSIANIC SYMBOLS

Besides the rather extensive portrayals of the Messiah in the Torah, other word pictures or symbols also gave the Jews a multi-faceted image of what He would be like:

1. Messiah was the "seed of the woman" (Gen. 3:15). The first biblical prophecy about the Messiah promised He would be supernaturally conceived— not the seed of a man but of a woman. Luke 1:26-35 records the fulfillment of that promise. The Seed would also battle Satan, bruising the Serpent's head, the place of a mortal wound.

2. Messiah was the "seed of Abraham" (Gen. 22:18). God confirmed His covenant with the promise that all the nations of earth would be blessed through Abraham's seed (not seeds). Matthew 1:1 and Galatians 3:14–16 record the fulfillment of that promise.

3. Messiah was "Shiloh" (Gen. 49:10–11). The reference to Judah's royal line, consummating in the king and lawgiver, was a prophecy with threefold significance: first, Messiah would be from the tribe of Judah; second, Messiah would be a lawgiver of royal stock; third, Messiah's person would attract multitudes (see Matt. 2:1–6; 5:1–12).

4. Messiah was the "Star of Jacob" (Num. 24:17–19). The "Star of Jacob" referred to a brilliant ruler unmatched by any other descendant of Jacob (see Rev. 19:11–16; 22:16).

5. Messiah was "Immanuel" (Isa. 7:13–14). Isaiah gave a threefold messianic promise: first, a son would be born of the house of David; second, the child would be conceived by a virgin; and third, the virgin-born son would possess deity as identified by His name—Immanuel, "God with us" (see Matt. 1:22–23).

6. Messiah was the "light to the Gentiles" (Isa. 60:1–5). The prophetic word said the "light" would come to a people in darkness and that light would be the glory of the Lord. Gentiles and kings would come to this "light" (see John 3:19–21; 8:12).

7. Messiah was the "ruler from Bethlehem" (Mic. 5:2). Micah's messianic prophecy not only set forth the village from which Messiah would come, but it also clearly described the ruler as having both an earthly and heavenly origin. He would be born as a child in Bethlehem, but His preexistence would be from eternity (see Matt. 2:1–6; John 8:56–58).

8. Messiah was the "desire of the nations" (Hag. 2:6–7). Haggai's prophecy indicated Messiah's second advent. Time would intervene between His first appearance and His second, with tribulation causing a desire for His coming (see 2 Thess. 1:5–10).

9. Messiah was the "branch" (Isa. 4:2–6; 11:1–10; Jer. 23:5–6; Zech. 3:8). The Messiah is presented as a branch growing out of the stump of David's family tree, the rod growing out of the stem of Jesse, David's father. He is a shoot off the stock of royalty. Jeremiah calls him the "Lord our Righteousness" (see Rev. 22:16).

10. Messiah is the "suffering servant" (Isa. 53). Torah pictures the Messiah as both the conquering, sovereign king as well as the suffering servant. His first appearance was as a humble redeemer who suffered for His people. His second appearance will reveal Him as the sovereign victor over all (see Matt. 27).

MESSIANIC PSALMS

Many of the Psalms contained references to the Messiah. Some references to David pointed to the coming king in David's family. Although many passages clearly spoke of a coming Messiah, others were veiled foreshadowings of the Anointed One. According to the New Testament, the following Psalms referred to Jesus as the Messiah:

1. "Thou art my Son; this day have I begotten thee" (Ps. 2:7b; see Acts 13:33).

2. "Thou hast put all things under his feet" (Ps. 8:6b; see Heb. 2:6–10).

3. "Thou wilt not leave my soul in hell, neither wilt thou suffer thine Holy One to see corruption" (Ps. 16:10; see Acts 2:27).

4. "My God, my God, why hast Thou forsaken me?" (Ps. 22:1a; see Matt. 27:46).

5. "He trusted on the LORD that he would deliver Him; let God deliver Him, seeing he delighted in him" (Ps. 22:8; see Matt. 27:43).

6. "They pierced my hands and my feet" (Ps. 22:16b; see John 20:25).

7. "They part my garments among them, and cast lots upon my vesture" (Ps. 22:18; see John 19:24).

8. "Lo, I am come . . . to do thy will, O my God." (Ps. 40:7–8; see Heb. 10:7).

9. "Yea, mine own familiar friend . . . which did eat of my bread, hath lifted up his heel against me" (Ps. 41:9; see John 13:18).

10. "For the zeal of thine house hath eaten me up" (Ps. 69:9a; see John 2:17).

11. "They gave me also gall . . . and in my thirst they gave me vinegar to drink" (Ps. 69:21; see Matt. 27:34, 48).

12. "And let another take his [the betrayer's] office" (Ps. 109:8b; see Acts 1:20).

13. "The LORD said unto my Lord, Sit thou at my right hand, until I make thine enemies thy footstool" (Ps. 110:1; see Matt. 22:44).

14. "The LORD hath sworn . . . Thou art a priest for ever after the order of Melchizedek" (Ps. 110:4; see Heb. 7:17).

15. "The stone which the builders refused is become the head stone of the corner" (Ps. 118:22; see Matt. 21:42).

16. "Blessed be he that cometh in the name of the LORD" (Ps. 118:26; see Matt. 21:9).

JEWISH VIEW OF MESSIAH AND MESSIANIC SIGNS

The First Sign: The Coming of Elijah

The Jews believe in a literal interpretation of Malachi 4:5–6, "Behold, I will send you Elijah, the prophet, before the coming of the great and dreadful day of the LORD; And he shall turn the heart of the fathers to the children, and the heart of the children to the fathers. . . ." To this day Jews earnestly pray and look for Elijah's appearance. His seat is still reserved in some ancient synagogues so that he can oversee the circumcisions of Jewish boys. His chair is prepared and left vacant at the Passover *Seder* table, just in case he should appear during the meal.

The rabbis believe that Elijah will assume the function of an arbitrator, judging legal matters that have not been settled. His messianic preparation will include settling disputes, and today Jews respond to unresolved difficulties with the advice, "put them aside until Elijah comes." But his primary responsibility is to prepare for a time of peace for the messianic kingdom.

Elijah will come not only as prophet and judge, but he will also come as a priest in the line of Aaron, Eleazar, and Phinehas. Elijah's priestly function will be to:

1. Bring a pot of manna that miraculously fed the Israelites in the wilderness. He will use this manna to feed the people during the woeful period before the Kingdom Age.

2. Bring a flask of water that miraculously flowed from the rock in the wilderness.

3. Bring a flask of oil that anointed the holy vessels and tabernacle in the wilderness. He will use this oil to anoint the Messiah.

4. Bring Aaron's rod that miraculously produced flowers and almonds in the wilderness. The rod will become Messiah's scepter.

The Second Sign: The Collapse of Human Government

> *And there shall be a time of trouble, such as never was since there was a nation even to that same time; and*

*at that time thy people shall be delivered, every one
that shall be found written in the book.*

(Dan. 12:1b)

Jews believe that social, moral, and economic collapse
will be the "birth pains" before Messiah's appearance.
War will spread, anarchy will prevail, and human society
will be in disarray. The chaos will affect not only
humanity but also nature. The rabbis said that blood
would ooze from the trees and the stones would cry out.
The intertestamental writer Baruch, writing in the
Apocalypse of Second Baruch 27:6 and following, describes the twelve woes that will come upon the earth
before the messianic age:

1. Commotions

2. Slayings of great ones

3. Many fall by death

4. The sword upon the earth

5. Famine and drought

6. Earthquakes and terrors

7. [Fragment left out of original]

8. Portents of fighting hordes (attacks)

9. The fall of fire

10. Repine and oppression

11. Wickedness and unchastity

12. Confusion and mingling of all the woes

Describing the woes of the earth before Messiah's advent, Baruch predicts that wonderment will come upon the people of the earth, torment will overtake them, and it will seem that God Himself has forgotten the earth. The rabbis expect that when humanity sinks to its lowest, Messiah will appear to bring the blessings of David's kingdom.

The Third Sign: Calculating the Time

> *The world shall last not less than eighty-five jubilees, and ben David shall appear in the last jubilee.*
>   (The Talmud, Sanhedrin 97b)

Calculating the date of Messiah's coming has been a sign, even though it is an unreliable one. Several rabbis have used complex calculations to try to determine the specific date of Messiah's arrival, but date setting has proved to be unsuccessful. In fact, the Talmud warns against such efforts: "There are seven things hidden from men. The day of death; the day of consolation; the extent of judgment; no man knows what is in the mind of his friend; man knows not which of his business enterprises will be profitable; or when the kingdom of David's house will be destroyed; or when the wicked kingdom will fall" (The Talmud, Pesahim 54b).

The Fourth Sign: Deeds of Repentance

The rabbis also taught that the total repentance of Israel was a precondition for Messiah's coming. They believed that human sin was holding back the Messiah, and until sin was expiated through penitence, prayer, study of Torah, and charity, He would not come. Rabbis firmly believed that redemption would follow repentance. Rabbi Jose the Galilean taught, "Great is repentance, because it brings redemption near."

The Fifth Sign: Deeds of Charity

The rabbis taught that the "birth pains" of Messiah (the time of tribulation) could be eased and Messiah's appearance could be hastened by studying the Torah and practicing charity. Rabbis believed that a return to the basic deeds of charity found in the Torah was a necessary prerequisite to Messiah's coming.

Although the Jews had many references to Messiah in the Torah, the rabbis also added to and elaborated on the Jewish picture of what Messiah would be like. The Hebrew people believed that Messiah would establish his kingdom on earth, bringing a perpetual sabbath for Israel and blessings for the Gentiles who accepted the unity of God and embraced His Torah.

But because of the rabbis' teaching, the Jews never believed that the Messiah would be divine, God Incarnate, or the Son of God. Throughout history the Jews believed that Messiah would be an ordinary man with no degree of deity. According to the Talmud, "If a man says, 'I am God,' he lies; if he says, 'I am the Son of God,' he will regret it; and if he says, 'I shall go into heaven,' he will utterly fail."

Jewish literature also presented a view of two Messiahs. The first was Mashiach ben David (Messiah, the son of David). He was characterized as a passive, humble, and kindly king who would establish the peaceful kingdom of David. Later in Jewish history, the rabbis developed another kind of Messiah called Mashiach ben Joseph (Messiah, the son of Joseph). He was a conquering warrior who would rid the nation of its enemies. The first view of Messiah was evident before the Babylonian exile. The later view followed the woes of the Babylonian exile and captivity, and it intensified with continuing Jewish persecution. Ultimately both concepts of Messiah were woven into rabbinic thought. Messiah would be first a conqueror and then a provider of world peace.

JESUS, THE MESSIAH

In spite of the rabbis' rejection, Jesus declared that all the Old Testament witnessed to His Messiahship (Luke 24:27; John 5:39). He said that the Law (or Moses), the Prophets, and the Writings (or Psalms) pointed to His Messiahship. He laid His hand on the whole collection of books, and declared that He, His death and resurrection, was in its substance.

The story of Jesus' life, from minor incidents to major events, was clearly foretold in the Torah. The fulfilled prophecy authenticated the genuineness of Jesus' claim, while giving evidence to the reality of God. The prophetic word of the Torah consummated in the Messiah Jesus.

Writing to the Jews, Matthew abundantly used quotations from the Torah to show the prophecies fulfilled in Jesus. With only a few exceptions, it is Matthew who points out Jesus' fulfillment of the following prophecies:

1. Messiah would be born of a virgin (Isa. 7:14; see Matt. 1:23).

2. Messiah would be born in Bethlehem (Mic. 5:2; see Matt. 2:6).

3. Messiah would sojourn in Egypt (Hos. 11:1; see Matt. 2:15).

4. Messiah would live in Galilee at Nazareth (Isa. 9:1–2; see Matt. 2:23; 4:15).

5. Messiah's coming would occasion the massacre of Bethlehem's children (Jer. 31:15; see Matt. 2:18).

6. Messiah's coming would be announced by a herald like Elijah (Isa. 40:3–5; Mal. 3:1; see Matt. 3:3–4).

7. Messiah would proclaim a Jubilee to the world (Isa. 61:1; see Luke 4:18–19).

8. Messiah's mission would include the Gentiles (Isa. 42:1–3, 6; see Matt. 12:18–21).

9. Messiah's ministry would be one of healing (Isa. 53:4–5; see Matt. 8:17).

10. Messiah would teach by using parables (Isa. 6:9–10; Ps. 78:1–2; see Matt. 13:14–15, 35).

11. Messiah would be disbelieved and rejected by the rulers (Isa. 29:13; 53:1; Pss. 69:4; 118:22; see Matt. 15:8–9; 21:42).

12. Messiah would make a triumphal entry into Jerusalem (Zech. 9:9; Ps. 118:26; see Matt. 21:5).

13. Messiah would be like a smitten shepherd (Zech. 13:7; see Matt. 26:31).

14. Messiah would be betrayed by a friend for thirty pieces of silver (Zech. 11:12–13; Ps. 41:9; see Matt. 27:9–10).

15. Messiah would die with the evil (Isa. 53:9, 12; see Matt. 27:44).

16. Messiah would be given vinegar and gall (Ps. 69:21; see Matt. 27:34).

17. Messiah would see His garments divided by lot (Ps. 22:18; see Matt. 27:35).

18. Messiah would have none of His bones broken (Num. 9:12; Ps. 34:20; see John 19:36).

19. Messiah would have His side, His hands, and His feet pierced (Zech. 12:10; Ps. 22:16; see John 19:37).

20. Messiah's dying words would repeat David's words (Pss. 22:1; 31:5; see Matt. 27:46).

21. Messiah would be buried by a rich man (Isa. 53:9; see Matt. 27:57–60).

22. Messiah's body would not decay (Ps. 16:10; see Matt. 27:63–64; 28:5–6).

FALSE MESSIAHS

Jewish history is filled with messianic pretenders, pseudo-messiahs, and outright false prophets. The following list provides a description of several would-be messiahs.

Theudas, A.D. 44. It is conceivable that there were two people named Theudas who pretended to be Messiah. The Theudas mentioned by Gamaliel in Acts 5:36 would have been an earlier one. Jewish history speaks of a Theudas who in A.D. 44 brought his followers to the banks of the Jordan River, promising to divide the waters in order to reveal his prophetic powers. But the Roman legion converged upon the group, crucified Theudas, and slew most of his followers.

The Egyptian (Acts 21:38). It is not known exactly when "the Egyptian" created the insurrection and proclaimed himself to be Messiah. Josephus informs us that the Egyptian gathered to himself thirty thousand followers and advanced to the Mount of Olives, desiring to overthrow the Roman garrison with his bodyguard of "Sicarii" (assassins). This false messiah had promised his deluded followers that he would cause the walls of Jerusalem to fall down (like those of Jericho). His "Sicarii" were a group of fanatical murderers who terrorized Jerusalem by carrying exposed daggers. They murdered whoever seemed obnoxious. In fact, they slew Jonathan, the high priest.

Simeon Bar Cochba, second century. Bar Cochba (son of a star) is perhaps one of the most well-known false messiahs. Due to his great charisma and military genius, Jewish warriors from all over the Mediterranean came to help him fight against the Romans. It is said that his army contained nearly a half-million warriors. Between A.D. 132 and 134, Bar Cochba defeated almost any enemies in his path. Sadly, it was the great rabbinic sage Rabbi Akiba ben Joseph who hailed Bar Cochba as the Messiah. And due to Rabbi Akiba's loyalty to Bar Cochba, 500,000 Jewish lives were lost in battle. Eventually when Bar Cochba had been defeated in A.D. 135, a Roman historian said, "All of Judea became almost a desert." The Jews were so disillusioned by Simeon Bar Cochba's failure that messianism, as the hope for the future deliverance, came to an end for centuries.

The capstone of all the Jewish false messiahs was Shabbatai Zevi, who in 1648, at a time when European Jews were intellectually illiterate, with supreme self-confidence, proclaimed himself Messiah ben David. When the Rabbinic Council of Smyrna heard of this outrageous claim they excommunicated Zevi. Nevertheless, he attracted large crowds. Because of his knowledge of the Talmud, he had become a rabbi at the age of eighteen. He had a musical voice and pleasing appearance. Zevi was known for his public displays, such as his public "marriage" to a scroll of the Torah, which outraged the rabbis and many in the Jewish community. But Zevi went a step further. He taught that sins that the Torah denounced could be "sanctified" and made a blessing. In essence, this self-acclaimed messiah taught that holy acts could be performed by sinning. His charisma was so pronounced that people flocked to him just to kiss his hand. He seemed to inspire mass hysteria, revelations, and visions wherever he went. At that time many Jews believed that the Messianic era was commencing. But the clamor calmed when Zevi was arrested by the Sultan and, to save his neck, became a Moslem in 1666. Sabbatai Zevi's name, and all it stands for, is for Jews what Judas Iscariot's name is for Christians.

Suffice it to say, there were scores of other Jewish pseudo-messiahs. Warning about the appearance of these false messiahs, Jesus said:

> *For there shall arise false Christs, and false prophets, and shall show great signs and wonders; insomuch that, if it were possible, they shall deceive the very elect. Behold, I have told you before. Wherefore if they shall say unto you, Behold, he is in the desert; go not forth: behold, he is in the secret chambers; believe it not. For as the lightning cometh out of the east, and shineth even unto the west; so shall also the coming of the Son of man be.*
>
> (Matt. 24:24–27)

Chapter 10

THE TORAH'S CURSED ONE

Scripture for study:

> *And if a man have committed a sin worthy of death, and he be put to death, and thou hang him on a tree, His body shall not remain all night upon the tree, but thou shalt in any wise bury him that day (for he that is hanged is accursed of God), that thy land be not defiled, which the LORD thy God giveth thee for an inheritance.*
>
> (Deut. 21:22–23)

> *And he made his grave with the wicked, and with the rich in his death, because he had done no violence, neither was any deceit in his mouth. Yet it pleased the LORD to bruise him; he hath put him to grief. When thou shalt make his soul an offering for sin, he shall see his seed, he shall prolong his days, and the pleasure of the LORD shall prosper in his hand.*
>
> (Isa. 53:9–10)

And after this Joseph, of Arimathea, being a disciple
of Jesus, but secretly for fear of the Jews, besought
Pilate that he might take away the body of Jesus; and
Pilate gave him leave. He came, therefore, and took
the body of Jesus. And there came also Nicodemus,
which at the first came to Jesus by night, and brought
a mixture of myrrh and aloes, about a hundred pound
weight. Then took they the body of Jesus, and wound
it in linen clothes with the spices, as the manner of the
Jews is to bury. Now in the place where he was
crucified there was a garden; and in the garden a new
sepulcher, wherein was never man yet laid.

(John 19:38–41)

Under the Torah, a man proven guilty of a capital
offense and put to death by stoning was displayed in
public. According to Deuteronomy 21:22, his body was to
"hang . . . on a tree," a grim object lesson to the
community that such a crime was a disgrace to humanity
and was not to be repeated. The transgressor's exposed
body also signaled the curse of God on the executed one:
"for he that is hanged is accursed of God" (Deut. 21:23c).
The term "hanged" did not refer to strangulation or
crucifixion, which were not allowed under the Torah or
practiced in Israel. The reference was strictly to public
exposure of the one executed.

Public display was not allowed beyond one day according to the Torah. The body must be buried by evening.
Deuteronomy 21:23 declared that if the body was left to
decay, it would bring defilement to the community: "But
thou shalt in any wise bury him that day . . . that thy land
be not defiled" (see also Josh. 8:29; 10:26–27).

Against this background of Mosaic law, Isaiah presented a paradox in his prophecy of Messiah. He said, "He was cut off out of the land of the living; for the transgression of my people was he stricken. And he made his grave with the wicked, and with the rich in his death, because he had done no violence, neither was any deceit in his mouth" (Isa. 53:8b–9). According to Isaiah, the Messiah would die a cursed death with the wicked (plural in this passage). But the words, "in his death," meaning "after death," referred to a burial with the rich (singular in this passage). The prophecy of Isaiah set forth the burial of the suffering servant as a sign: though He would be slain as a criminal, He would be buried as a wealthy and righteous man.

By the time of Jesus, Isaiah's prophetic requirements were somewhat difficult to fulfill. Under Roman domination the Jews did not have free rights to execute capital punishment. Also the Pharisees of Jesus' day were opposed to execution for any crime. According to one rabbinic expression, "A Sanhedrin which executes a person once in seven years may be called 'destructive.'" Rabbi-Sage Eliezer ben Azariah put it more tersely, "A Sanhedrin which executes a person once in seventy years can be called 'destructive.'" Rabbi Akiba and Rabbi Tarphon said, "Were we on the great Sanhedrin, no man would ever be put to death."

Jewish criminals were executed by Rome, usually by crucifixion. But the likelihood of proper burial following such a death was very slim. Criminals were left unburied, disgraced by interment in an unclean place, or carted off to the valley of Gehinnom (Gehenna) for cremation.

Nevertheless, Jesus fulfilled both Isaiah's prophecy and the requirements of the Torah in His death and burial. According to Peter, Jesus "his own self bare our sins in his own body on the tree . . ." (1 Peter 2:24a). With that, He received the curse of the Torah as Paul stressed, "Christ hath redeemed us from the curse of the law, being made a curse for us; for it is written, Cursed is every one that hangeth on a tree" (Gal. 3:13). Messiah experienced the shame of public exposure on a tree, the cross. But His body was also given burial before evening, fulfilling the Torah's requirement.

Jesus was condemned to die by the majority of Pharisees and Sadducees of the Sanhedrin. Since the Sadducees were not opposed to capital punishment and their party ruled the Sanhedrin, it is possible that they stacked the majority vote for execution. According to the Gospel record, however, the Pharisees agreed that Jesus should die (Matt. 27:1). They felt threatened. They hated Jesus, and they forsook their own cherished regulations to see Him executed.

Only a few Pharisees would not participate in the conspiracy against Jesus. Some of them, bent on justice, did not vote for execution or had dismissed their presence from the council. Probably Gamaliel, who later spoke for Peter and John (Acts 5:34–39), was not present. When Jesus' disciples scattered, two Pharisees—Joseph of Arimathea and Nicodemus, august members of the great Sanhedrin—were His burial society (John 19:38–39).

Both of these Pharisees were waiting for the kingdom of God; they were just men, set on righteousness (John 7:51). Both men were supremely interested in Jesus and secretly became His disciples. They did not wish excommunication from the synagogue, expulsion from the council, or ostracism from Jewish society.

According to John's record, Joseph exerted his courage by asking for Jesus' body. He "besought Pilate that he might take away the body of Jesus" (John 19:38c). That means Joseph pressed for it and appealed to the highest authority. As a friend he desired to give Jesus a decent and loving interment, and as a Pharisee he was obedient to the Torah's injunction to remove the body before sundown.

Rabbi Nicodemus, a "ruler of the Jews" (John 3:1, 10), collaborated with Joseph on the arrangement of the costly burial. Nicodemus supplied one hundred pounds of burial spices, while Joseph purchased the linen shroud and donated his own garden tomb.

To understand the reasons why Joseph and Nicodemus undertook such a burial, we should briefly examine their role as Pharisees. Flavius Josephus describes the Pharisees this way:

> [They] ascribe all things to fate and God, yet allow that to do what is right or the contrary is principally in man's own power, although fate cooperates in every action.
>
> They think that every soul is immortal; only the souls of good men will pass into another body, but the souls of the evil shall suffer everlasting punishment—they believe that under the earth there will be rewards or punishments, according as they have lived virtuously or viciously in this life, and the latter are to be detained in an everlasting prison, but that the former shall have the power to revive and live again.
>
> They interpret the law [Torah] with careful exactitude.

The Pharisees also maintained Messianic hopes for Israel when their rivals were giving in to the Romans. Their great imagination for the Messianic future aided the faith of the common people who were then better able to understand Jesus and his Messianic claims.

The Talmud gives a seven-fold characterization of the Pharisees, which confirms the Gospel representation:

1. The "shoulder" Pharisee—who wears his good deeds on his shoulders and obeys the precepts of the Law, not from principle, but from expediency.

2. The "wait-a-little" Pharisee—who begs for time to perform a meritorious act.

3. The "bleeding" Pharisee—who in his eagerness to avoid looking on a woman, shuts his eyes and bruises himself to bleeding by stumbling against a wall.

4. The "painted" Pharisee—who advertises his holiness lest anyone should touch him and defile him.

5. The "reckoning" Pharisee—who is always saying, "What duty must I do to balance any unpalatable duty which I have neglected?"

6. The "fearing" Pharisee—whose relation to God is one merely of trembling awe.

7. The Pharisee for "Love." In all but the last there is the element of acting, of hypocrisy.

Such Pharisees as Nicodemus and Joseph, met this seventh class. Only love could have guided them in the burial of Messiah.

It has been the belief of Jews since the Pharisee sages that burial is to be with dignity. Belief in the resurrection of the body gave impetus to carefully treat the body and give it proper interment. Jews believe it will rise again for the last judgment and eternal life at the end of days. Care is taken against any physical injury so when the Messiah blows the *shofar* (see 1 Thess. 4:16–17) the body will rise without former damages to be reunited with the soul. The burial of Jesus probably followed this ancient pattern of burial:

1. The body is thoroughly washed as a purification rite.

2. It is placed on a white sheet on the purification "board."

3. "Forgiveness" is asked of the body for the intimate job of washing.

4. Washed and dried it is wrapped in a linen shroud.

5. If inside, the feet were always pointed toward the door.

6. The palms of the hands were always left open—the fingers never closed.

7. The eyes and mouth were covered with coins and potsherds to prevent demons from entering the body.

8. The white-shroud wrapped body is put directly in the grave in some countries.

9. The plain pine coffin, without metal, glued at the joints, is used by the Orthodox.

10. Under the head is placed a little sack of earth from Israel, and some is sprinkled on the body.

11. The name of the person is called out in Hebrew so he will not forget it until Messiah calls his name for resurrection. (See John 5:25.)

12. The resurrection dead will arise to face Mount Zion.

In Jesus' case, the spices were abundant and expensive. The myrrh (an incense gum) and aloes (a fragrant wood) were ground up and spread over the body and among the folds of the shroud. Joseph and Nicodemus insured that in spite of Jesus' illegal and cursed death, His burial was timely, according to the Torah, and richly performed, according to Isaiah's prophecy.

Chapter 11

THE TORAH'S MELCHIZEDEK PRIEST

Scripture for study:

An early, somewhat obscure incident in the Torah told the story of Melchizedek:

> *And Melchizedek, king of Salem, brought forth bread and wine; and he was the priest of the most high God. And he blessed him, and said, Blessed be Abram of the most high God, possessor of heaven and earth: And blessed be the most high God, which hath delivered thine enemies into thy hand. And he gave him tithes of all.*
>
> (Gen. 14:18–20)

Upon Abram's victory over the Mesopotamian kings and his rescue of Lot, Melchizedek met him at ancient Jerusalem (Salem), bringing bread and wine. Apparently these refreshments were also spiritual symbols since Melchizedek followed their presentation with a priestly blessing. Abram responded by acknowledging Melchizedek's greatness and offering the priest tithes of all he possessed. Following their exchange Melchizedek vanished into inscrutable seclusion. The Torah made no further reference to his origin, his continuing ministry, or his end. The author of the story did not describe Melchizedek's parents or the rest of his genealogy—a change of style from the rest of the book. His life was a mystery, although several things were apparent.

Melchizedek's name meant "king of righteousness." He was probably a Canaanitish prince-chieftan-priest who retained the true faith in God during the darkness of early heathenism. Since he ruled and ministered in Salem (ancient Jerusalem), he was also called "king of peace" (Salem meant "peace"). Thus incorporated in this godly man were the dual offices of priest and king.

Melchizedek's priesthood preceded the Levitical priesthood by approximately four centuries. In his priestly service the elements of later Levitical practice were already present. His blessing on Abram precipitated Abraham's blessing on Isaac (Gen. 25:5), Isaac's blessing on Jacob (Gen. 28:1-4), and Jacob's blessing on his children (Gen. 49:28). Melchizedek's gifts of bread and wine not only became symbols of provision and joy from God but they also were later used in sacrifice on the tabernacle altar. Based on Abram's tithe to Melchizedek, Moses later incorporated into the Levitical system the practice of tithing (Lev. 27:30-33; Num. 18:21-32).

Unlike the Levitical system, however, Melchizedek's priesthood apparently never ended. The Levites' service had a definite commencement and conclusion; without a temple and altar they could not properly function. Their priesthood depended on carnal ceremonies, but Melchizedek's rested on the power of a holy character. Melchizedek's priesthood as king of righteousness and king of peace foreshadowed a better priesthood—the priesthood of Messiah who would abide a priest perpetually.

MELCHIZEDEK IN THE PSALMS

Psalm 110 was the only link between the original story of Melchizedek in Genesis 14 and the explanation of Messiah's priesthood in Hebrews 7:

> The LORD said unto my Lord, Sit thou at my right hand, until I make thine enemies thy footstool. The LORD shall send the rod of thy strength out of Zion; rule thou in the midst of thine enemies. Thy people shall be willing in the day of thy power; in the beauties of holiness from the womb of the morning, thou hast the dew of thy youth. The LORD hath sworn, and will not repent, Thou art a priest for ever after the order of Melchizedek.
>
> (Ps. 110:1–4)

The psalm set forth four distinct revelations: First, David addressed Messiah as "my Lord," pointing to the Anointed One's separate identity as well as His superior position. Second, David referred to Messiah's royalty in the words, "thy strong scepter from Zion." Third, David recorded the oath of God that Messiah's priesthood would follow the manner of Melchizedek and not the Levitical priests. Finally, David indicated that Messiah's priesthood would be universal and unending. Essentially David's psalm declares that Messiah would be Lord, King, and Priest.

Psalm 110 made a particularly strong statement because

it contained divine oath, solemnly given. By His own character and His name, God pledged to fulfill His word. This irrevocable decree was made still more impressive by the added assurance that He "will not repent." Intertwined with the sacredness of God's name, the union of the royal and priestly offices in the Messiah was guaranteed.

Jesus later interpreted the psalm for the Pharisees and said that David called Him Lord:

> *While the Pharisees were gathered together, Jesus asked them, Saying, What think ye of Christ? whose son is he? They say unto him, The son of David. He saith unto them, How, then, doth David, in spirit, call him Lord, saying, The LORD said unto my Lord, Sit thou on my right hand, till I make thine enemies thy footstool? If David, then, call him Lord, how is he his son? And no man was able to answer him a word, neither durst any man from that day forth ask him any more questions.*
>
> (Matt. 22:41–46)

JESUS, A PRIEST LIKE MELCHIZEDEK

Three short verses introduced Melchizedek in Genesis. One thousand years later a single verse, Psalm 110:4, pointed to a Messiah who would be a priest like Melchizedek. After another thousand years a chapter in Hebrews explained that Jesus was the priest foretold in prophecy:

> *Now consider how great this man was, unto whom even the patriarch, Abraham, gave the tenth of the spoils. And verily they that are of the sons of Levi,*

who receive the office of the priesthood, have a commandment to take tithes of the people according to the law, that is, of their brethren, though they come out of the loins of Abraham; But he whose descent is not counted from them received tithes of Abraham, and blessed him that had the promises. And without all contradiction the less is blessed of the better. And here men that die receive tithes; but there he receiveth them, of whom it is witnessed that he liveth. And as I may so say, Levi also, who receiveth tithes, payed tithes in Abraham. For he was yet in the loins of his father, when Melchizedek met him.

(Heb. 7:4–10)

The author of the epistle used typical rabbinic style to argue Melchizedek's superior priesthood. First, his priesthood was better because it was perpetual. The phrase, "men that die receive tithes," pointed out the mortality of the Levites. Since the Genesis record did not mention the death of Melchizedek, the rabbis would typically conclude that he was still alive. He would be recognized as a perpetual priest who was still receiving tithes through Abraham's descendants.

Second, Melchizedek could claim a higher priesthood because the Levites themselves had paid him homage. According to Jewish tradition, the entire Torah, its priesthood and ordinances, was believed to be in Abraham because he was the father of the nation. All of his descendants were "in his loins" during his lifetime as well. Therefore, following typical Hebrew reasoning, Levi was in the loins of father Abraham when Abraham paid tithes to Melchizedek. Melchizedek, then, was greater than Levi.

The author of Hebrews continued:

> *If, therefore, perfection were by the Levitical priest-
> hood (for under it the people received the law), what
> further need was there that another priest should rise
> after the order of Melchizedek, and not be called after
> the order of Aaron? For the priesthood being changed,
> there is made of necessity a change also of the law. For
> he of whom these things are spoken pertaineth to
> another tribe, of which no man gave attendance at the
> altar. For it is evident that our Lord sprang out of
> Judah, of which tribe Moses spake nothing concerning
> priesthood. And it is yet far more evident; for that
> after the similitude of Melchizedek there ariseth
> another priest, Who is made, not after the law of a
> carnal commandment but after the power of an
> endless life. For he testifieth, Thou art a priest for ever
> after the order of Melchizedek.*
>
> (Heb. 7:11–17)

An institution is perfect if it effects the purpose for
which it was instituted. The purpose of the Levitical
priesthood was to remove sin and its consequences,
providing both forgiveness and access to God. However,
the Levitical priesthood could do this only symbolically.
Because the sacrifices could not actually remove sin and
provide salvation, a new priesthood had to be instituted.
That new priesthood was foreplanned by God, using
Melchizedek as the type. Since the Levitical priesthood
brought nothing to completion, another priest from
another order was needed.

The Hebrew priests were chosen because they were
born into a particular family. If a man fulfilled the proper

external requirements, no matter how spiritually ill-suited for the office he was, the Torah made him a priest. It was the carnal commandment, their physical pedigree, that made them priests. They functioned in response to external laws. But Melchizedek was different. He functioned by the power of a holy life, a life "in the Spirit."

Likewise, Messiah performed his duties, not after a carnal commandment but by the Spirit's compulsion and through a holy life. Death could not dissolve His priesthood, for it was confirmed by His resurrection. Unlike the Levitical priesthood, Messiah's priesthood is eternal. This Priest took His seat in heaven. His sacrificial work is finished. He is now the High Priest in the heavenly tabernacle, unlike Aaron who could officiate only in an earthly one. Messiah, then, is superior to Aaron because He serves in a better sanctuary. Since Messiah was not a priest after the order of Aaron, He could not perform priestly service on earth, for the Law would not allow it. But the Priest after the order of Melchizedek is allowed to be a continual High Priest in heaven itself. Messiah's priesthood was superior to Aaron's because:

1. Messiah's priesthood was royal.

2. Messiah's priesthood was initiated by God's oath.

3. Messiah was sinless.

4. Messiah's priesthood was nontransferable.

5. Messiah never dies.

6. Messiah's priesthood is everlasting.

PRIESTS TODAY

Orthodox Judaism still looks forward to the temple's restoration on Mount Zion. Jewish law, acknowledging the ruin of the temple and the scattering of all the ministering priests, allows the priests' male descendants to maintain Levitical purity and a degree of priestly duties. Genealogy must still be kept and a pedigreed priesthood must be preserved until the coming of Messiah. The priests' direct male descendants must always be ready to once again lead the nation in worship. Orthodox Jews believe that temple worship will be restored during future messianic times. In traditional Jewish thinking, the destruction of the temple and banishment of the priests by no means annuls the prospects of a continued ministry.

From the Christian point of view, the Levitical priesthood has been superseded by the priesthood of Messiah. But from the Jewish point of view, the Levitical priesthood continues. In synagogues all over the world, the descendants of the ancient priests are required by law to perform certain duties. Genealogically, Jews are divided into three groups:

1. The priests (*Cohanim*)

2. The Levites (assistants to the priests)

3. The Israelites (the national group of all others)

Today the priest (*cohen*) has the privilege to conduct the ritual for the redemption of the first-born son (*Pidyon Haben*), to publicly read the Torah, and to pronounce the priestly benediction. His lawful duty is to bless the people at the conclusion of the synagogue service. There are, however, disqualifying restrictions on a Cohen as found in the Torah. He is ineligible to perform priestly duties if in violation of the following requirements:

1. If he is drunk or has consumed alcoholic beverage which is still in his system prior to pronouncing the benediction.

2. If he is physically deformed or has any physical blemishes.

3. If he has married a divorced woman.

4. If he is the son of a Cohen whose marriage was in violation of the Torah.

5. If he has come into contact with the dead; in the same room or within six feet of a grave.

6. He cannot be a mourner before burial takes place in order to pronounce the Benediction, nor a mourner for his father or mother during the twelve months of mourning. If, however, there are no other priests in the synagogue to pronounce the benediction, he may do so, but not during the special seven days of mourning after death.

7. If he has committed a murder, even after sorrow, repentance, and punishment. He has forfeited his right to be a priest.

8. If he is detested by the synagogue or if he despises them.

It is not only a requirement but a commandment for the Cohen to bless the people of Israel (Num. 6:23). When he is called to the platform for the priestly benediction, he is expected to perform his duty. If he is unqualified for the above reasons he will politely leave the synagogue before that point so he will not be in violation of the Torah.

Before the ritual of benediction is performed, the Cohen must purify himself for the Psalm says, "Lift up thy hands in holiness and bless ye the Lord" (Ps. 134:2). The Cohen must first wash his hands up to his wrists. He is to be assisted by a Levite. The Levite pours the water over the into a ritual laver. The Cohen has taken his shoes off because when he pronounces the benediction he is standing on holy ground. This aspect of the ritual comes from Moses. When Moses stood before the Lord he removed his shoes. He will then come solemnly toward the Holy Ark where the scrolls of the Torah are stored. He will stand on the steps before it and cover his head with his prayer shall. The Reader calls out the words of the benediction and the Cohen repeats them, chanting. His hands are raised, palms facing downward, thumbs tip to tip, and the first finger joining the second, and the third finger joining the fourth. He is not allowed to look at his own hands, nor is the congregation allowed to look upon them. Tradition has it that at that moment the Glory of God rests upon the Cohen's hands and could have a blinding effect upon the eyes. Pious Jews will shut their eyes tight or bury their heads during the benediction.

The words of the benediction are exactly as they were in ancient times:

The Lord bless thee and keep thee;
The Lord make his face to shine upon
    thee and be gracious unto thee.
The Lord lift up His countenance upon
    thee and give thee peace.

Another duty of the modern Cohen is to be the officiant of the service of *Pidyon Haben* (redemption of the son). It is one of the few responsibilities of the Jewish priests today. Only a Cohen qualifies for this service, but the responsibility of redeeming the son belongs to the father. It should take place on the thirty-first day after birth, although if for some reason the father delays, he is under obligation to have it performed until the boy is thirteen. After that time the son must redeem himself.

The father brings his first-born son to the Cohen and tells him that he is the first-born of his mother. The child is placed on a table, on a pillow. Then an ancient dialogue takes place between the Cohen and the father. The father places five silver dollars beside the child, in keeping with the Torah's injunction about five shekels for the price of redemption. The money is taken by the father and he says: "Blessed art thou, Lord our God, King of the Universe who has sanctified us with His Commandments and commanded us concerning the redemption of the first-born son." He then gives the money to the Cohen. The Cohen passes it over the son's head with the words of the ritual. He puts the money down, then with hands over the son's head pronounces the Levitical benediction. The ritual is completed with a cup of wine and blessing.

The intent of the ritual formula is extended beyond the rite of redemption. It is accompanied with the hope that the son might be destined to adhere to the Torah as he grows up, be blessed with a good marriage, and live a life of good deeds.

The Cohen is an official representative of his geneological forebears who performed the service in ancient times.

Unlike the priests of almost all religions who conduct burial for the dead, the Jewish Cohen is forbidden by the Torah to even come near a corpse (Lev. 21: 1–4). Probably the reason for this is that in ancient times the heathen Canaanite priests practiced death-cult rites. The priests of Moloch made children pass through the fire, and human sacrifice was practiced by Israel's neighbors. Thus, by command of God, Israel's priests were not to touch a dead person. The one service rendered by Christian ministers, funerals, and burials, cannot be performed by Jewish priests.

The priest was forbidden to defile himself and was was strickly required to maintain ritual purity. He could not enter a house where the dead lay, nor could he enter a burial ground. With modifications, this regulation is still in force today. Even under the open sky, a Cohen is prohibited from coming any closed than six feet from a grave. According to Talmudic law, however, he can come fifteen inches from a body if it is being carried to burial.

According to the Torah, he is permitted to "defile" himself for the sake of burying his own loved ones. In this case, it is expected that he would assist in the funeral and burial.

Since historic Judaism seeks to perpetuate the Levitical priesthood (which in reality has been superseded by the death and resurrection of Messiah), both the *cohanim* and the Levites come under the stern indictments of the following passage:

And now, O ye priests, this commandment is for you. If ye will not hear, and if ye will not lay it to heart, to give glory unto my name, saith the LORD of hosts, I will even send a curse upon you, and I will curse your blessings: yea, I have cursed them already, because ye do not lay it to heart. Behold, I will corrupt your seed, and spread dung upon your faces, even the dung of your solemn feasts; and one shall take you away with it. And ye shall know that I have sent this commandment unto you, that my covenant might be with Levi, saith the LORD of hosts. My covenant was with him of life and peace; and I gave them to him for the fear wherewith he feared me, and was afraid before my name. The law of truth was in his mouth, and iniquity was not found in his lips: he walked with me in peace and equity, and did turn many away from iniquity. For the priest's lips should keep knowledge, and they should seek the law at his mouth: for he is the messenger of the LORD of hosts. But ye are departed out of the way; ye have caused many to stumble at the law; ye have corrupted the covenant of Levi, saith the LORD of hosts. Therefore have I also made you contemptible and base before all the people, according as ye have not kept my ways, but have been partial in the law.

(Mal. 2:1–9)

Malachi said the ancient priests had corrupted the covenant that God had made with Levi. Since they broke their part of the covenant, God was no longer bound by it. Since they did not pay Him due reverence, He withdrew His promised blessings to Levi. The honor and glory of the Levitical priesthood was turned into disgrace and contempt. The Torah said, "Them that honor me I will honor, and they that despise me shall be lightly esteemed" (1 Sam. 2:30b). The prophet Malachi pointed out the one gross sin of the Levitical priests: they had not kept the Lord's ways but had been partial in the administration of the Torah. From Malachi's perspective as one of the last prophets, he viewed the whole scope of past Levitical ministry and clearly set forth the failure of the Jewish priesthood. They had faltered. And so have all their descendants. The obvious need was for a new priesthood, established upon a holy character rather than upon the carnal commandment for a pedigreed ministry. Thus, in the Messiah, the Levitical order ceased, for the covenant made with Levi was set aside by the Lord.

Chapter 12

THE TORAH'S LION

Scripture for study:

When the aged Jacob (Israel) was ready to die, he spoke a blessing over his son Judah. Jacob had faced rigorous trials, failures, sorrows, and some successes. But now at life's summit, he was exalted at the prospects of his children's futures as he saw how he would live in his children:

> *Judah, thou art he whom thy brethren shall praise: thy hand shall be in the neck of thine enemies; thy father's children shall bow down before thee. Judah is a lion's whelp: from the prey, my son, thou art gone up: he stooped down, he crouched as a lion, and as an old lion. Who shall rouse him up? The scepter shall not depart from Judah, nor a lawgiver from between his feet, until Shiloh come; and unto him shall the gathering of the people be.*

> (Gen. 49:8–12)

Jacob, with a bold and striking symbol, compared his son Judah to a young lion. He described him growing into full strength and ferocity, roaming through the deserts in search of prey, then returning to his wilderness den. Jacob portrayed his comfortable majesty after the prey was eaten—crouching in security and masterful serenity. Jacob's prophecy envisioned Judah as a courageous, invincible son and hero. As a gifted prophet, Jacob's picture went beyond his immediate son to one of his future descendants who would possess all these characteristics of royalty.

Although the lion is no longer found in Palestine, it roamed the earth in Jacob's time, inhabiting Syria, Asia Minor, and the Balkans. Among the ancient Egyptians, Babylonians, Assyrians, and Hebrews, the lion stood as a symbol of strength, courage, and ferocity. Among the Jews, the lion later represented the house of David and the line of Judah.

Since the image of the lion was so strongly associated with the house of David, the rabbis allowed its use on Jewish art objects without its condemnation as an idol. An ancient seal depicting the lion was excavated at Megiddo. The lion of Judah appeared on the seal of *Shema*, a servant of Jeroboam (about 933 B.C.). The symbol of the lion was also displayed on the banner of Judah's tribe in ancient times. Later it was found on synagogue architecture and decorations. Even today lions are often embroidered on Torah mantels, engraved in silver for the Torah's breastplate, or sewn into the tapestry of the curtain concealing the ark. Most often lions are portrayed flanking the crown of the Torah. In ceremonial art they are displayed facing one another as indicative of royalty beholding the Divine.

Besides displaying the visual imagery of lions, the Jews

built up an extensive folklore and rabbinic tradition about the animals. The talmudic literature included the following ideas:

1. The sound of God's voice was like the roar of a lion.

2. Lions became angry with Noah aboard the ark and suffered fever because they were shorted their daily ration.

3. Noah slew a lion in a vineyard, mingling its blood with the soil. Therefore, when a man drank wine, he became as strong as a lion.

4. Judah the son of Jacob was properly called "a lion's whelp" because he had the facial features of a lion.

5. Moses had the power to tame the lions guarding the palace of Pharaoh.

6. Solomon had special power over lions and used lions as servants in his palace.

7. Daniel had the power to make lions docile, but when Nebuchadnezzar changed into a beast, he changed into a lion for seven years.

The Israelites also saw the lion as a messianic image. They expected a conquering Messiah—a man of war like David—who would subdue their enemies and mete out final judgment. One rabbinic vision said, "How beautiful is the Messiah King, who is about to rise from Judah's house. He has bound his lions and gone forth to battle against those who hate him; princes and kings shall be slain; he will make red the rivers with the blood of the slain—his garments will be dipped in blood."

Apocryphal literature added,

> *As for the lion whom thou didst see roused from the wood and roaring, and speaking to the eagle [believed to be the Roman Empire], and reproving him for his unrighteousness and all his deeds, as thou hast heard; This is the Messiah whom the Most High hath kept unto the end of the days, who shall spring from the seed of David, and shall come and speak unto them; he shall reprove them for their ungodliness, rebuke them for their unrighteousness, reproach them to their faces with their treacheries.*
>
> (4 Esdras 12:31–32)

JESUS, JUDAH'S LION

Although Jesus was characterized in the Scriptures as "the Lamb of God," He was also named Victor, Judge, and royal, triumphant Lion. Jesus reflected His compassion and gentleness in His first advent as the world's redeemer. But according to the Book of Revelation, Jesus will yet return to judge this world. He will be the Lion of Judah's tribe. A victorious Jesus will bring the existing world order to an end, not as the Lamb of God but as the Lion of Judah. His hand will be on the neck of His enemies:

> *And I saw in the right hand of him that sat on the throne a book written within and on the backside, sealed with seven seals. And I saw a strong angel*

proclaiming with a loud voice, Who is worthy to open
the book, and to loose the seals thereof? And no man
in heaven, nor in earth, neither under the earth, was
able to open the book, neither to look thereon. And I
wept much, because no man was found worthy to
open and to read the book, neither to look thereon.
And one of the elders saith unto me, Weep not;
behold, the Lion of the tribe of Judah, the Root of
David, hath prevailed to open the book, and to loose
the seven seals thereof.

(Rev. 5:1–5)

In this scene, a prelude to the termination of the
present world and Satan's rule, an angel cried for
someone to open God's book of future secrets. Although
no one was at first found worthy to open the scroll, a
heavenly elder finally announced that the Lion of the tribe
of Judah had prevailed to break the seals and open the
scroll. Surprisingly, though, when John turned to see the
Lion of Judah, he saw a lamb instead: "And I beheld and,
lo, in the midst of the throne and of the four beasts, and
in the midst of the elders, stood a Lamb as if it had been
slain . . ." (Rev. 5:6).

In this passage John brought together the Torah's Lion
and the Torah's Paschal Lamb. According to John's
revelation, Jesus' sacrifice as the Lamb was completed.
But His return as the Lion Warrior was yet to be carried
out. John went on to predict that the Lion and the Lamb
will return as King of Kings and Lord of Lords:

And I saw heaven opened and, behold, a white horse;
and he that sat upon him was called Faithful and
True, and in righteousness he doth judge and make

war. His eyes were as a flame of fire, and on his head were many crowns; and he had a name written, that no man knew, but he himself. And he was clothed with a vesture dipped in blood; and his name is called The Word of God. And the armies which were in heaven followed him upon white horses, clothed in fine linen, white and clean. And out of his mouth goeth a sharp sword, that with it he should smite the nations, and he shall rule them with a rod of iron; and he treadeth the winepress of the fierceness and wrath of Almighty God. And he hath on his vesture and on his thigh a name written, KING OF KINGS, AND LORD OF LORDS.

(Rev. 19:11–16)

Jesus will one day wear the crown of Judah and the diadem of David. And in due time, all Israel will recognize Him according to Jacob's prophecy that He would be praised by His brethren.

Jesus eternally will be the perfect crown of the most holy law ever given. He initiated it, kept it, fulfilled it, and forgives our insolent and ignorant violations of it. Jesus is the Lion of Judah, the Son of David, the Crown of the Torah!

> "Look, ye saints, the sight is glorious:
>   See the Man of Sorrows now;
> From the fight returned Victorious,
>   Every knee to him shall bow:
>   Crown Him! Crown Him!
>   Crowns become the victor's brow.

"Sinners in derision crowned him
    Mocking thus Messiah's claim;
Saints and angels throng around him,
    Own his title, praise his Name:
    Crown him! Crown him!
        Spread abroad the victor's fame.

"Hark! those bursts of acclamation;
    Hark! those loud triumphant chords,
Jesus takes the highest station;
    O what joy the sight affords.
    Crown him! Crown him!
        King of Kings and Lord of Lords."

                                Thomas Kelly, 1809

BIBLIOGRAPHY

Ausubel, Nathan. *The Book of Jewish Knowledge.* New York: Crown Publishers, 1964.

Barclay, William. *The Gospel of John.* Philadelphia: The Westminster Press, 1956.

_____. *The Gospel of Luke.* Philadelphia: The Westminster Press, 1956.

_____. *The Gospel of Mark.* Philadelphia: The Westminster Press, 1957.

_____. *The Gospel of Matthew, Volume 1.* Philadelphia: The Westminster Press, 1958.

_____. *The Letter to the Romans.* Philadelphia: The Westminster Press, 1960.

Buksbazen, Victor. *The Gospel in the Feasts of Israel.* Fort Washington, Pa.: Christian Literature Crusade, 1954.

Buttrick, George Arthur (ed.). *The Interpreter's Bible: General Articles on the New Testament, Matthew, Mark.* New York: Abingdon Press, 1951.

_____. *The Interpreter's Bible: Luke, John.* New York: Abingdon Press, 1951.

Carroll, B.H. *An Interpretation of the English Bible: Leviticus.* Nashville: Broadman Press, 1947.

Chadwick, George Alexander. *The Expositor's Bible, The Book of Exodus.* New York: A.C. Armstrong Co., 1903. Reprinted, Grand Rapids: Baker Book House.

Dauermann, Stuart. "Y'Shua, Why That Name?" *Issues,* Vol. 3. Hineni Ministries, 1982.

Dods, Marcus. *The Expositor's Bible, Genesis.* New York: A.C. Armstrong Co., 1903. Reprinted, Grand Rapids: Baker Book House.

Donin, Hayim H. *To Be a Jew.* New York: Basic Books, 1972.

The Encyclopedia Judaica Jerusalem. New York: The Macmillan Company, 1972.

Gibson, John Monro. *The Expositor's Bible, Gospel of Saint Matthew.* New York: A.C. Armstrong Co., 1903. Reprinted, Grand Rapids: Baker Book House.

Gross, David C. *The Jewish People's Almanac.* New York: Doubleday & Co., Inc., 1981.

Henry, Matthew. *Deuteronomy, Volume 1.* New York: Fleming H. Revell Company.

———. *Exodus, Volume 1.* New York: Fleming H. Revell Company.

———. *John, Volume 8.* New York: Fleming H. Revell Company.

———. *Matthew, Volume 5.* New York: Fleming H. Revell Company.

Ironside, H.A. *Lectures on the Book of Revelation.* Neptune, N.J.: Loizeaux Brothers Inc., 1920.

Kellogg, Samuel Henry. *The Expositor's Bible, The Book of Leviticus.* New York: A.C. Armstrong Co., 1903. Reprinted, Grand Rapids: Baker Book House.

Knight, Walter B. *Three Thousand Illustrations for Christian Service.* Grand Rapids: Wm. B. Eerdmans Publishing Company, 1954.

Levi, Shonie B, and Kaplan, Sylvia R. *The Guide for the Jewish Homemaker.* New York: Schocken Books Inc., 1959.

Levitt, Zola. *The Seven Feasts of Israel.* 1979.

McCall, Thomas and Levitt, Zola. *Satan in the Sanctuary.* Chicago: Moody Press, 1973.

Maclaren, Alexander. *Expositions of Holy Scripture, John.* New York: George H. Doran Co. Reprinted, Grand Rapids: Baker Book House.

_____. *Expositions of Holy Scripture, Leviticus.* New York: George H. Doran Co. Reprinted, Grand Rapids: Baker Book House.

_____. *Expositions of Holy Scripture, Matthew.* New York: George H. Doran Co. Reprinted, Grand Rapids: Baker Book House.

_____. *Expositions of Holy Scripture, Psalms.* New York: George H. Doran Co. Reprinted, Grand Rapids: Baker Book House.

Maimonides, Moses ben. *Mishneh Torah.* Translated by Philip Birnbaum. New York: Hebrew Publishing Co., 1974.

Morgan, G. Campbell. *The Gospel According to Matthew.* New York: Fleming H. Revell Company, 1929.

Orr, James (gen. ed.). *The International Standard Bible Encyclopedia, Vol 4.* Chicago: The Howard-Severance Co., 1925. Reprinted, Grand Rapids: Wm. B. Eerdmans Publishing Company.

Rosen, Moishe. *Christ in the Passover.* Chicago: Moody Press, 1978.

Seigel, Richard, and Rheins, Carl. *The Jewish Almanac.* New York: Bantam Books, 1980.

Singer, Isidore (ed.). *The Jewish Encyclopedia.* New York: Funk and Wagnalls Co., 1912.

Spence-Jones, H. D. M. (ed.). *The Pulpit Commentary, Deuteronomy (Series 6).* W. L. Alexander, expositor. New York: Funk & Wagnalls Co. Reprinted, Grand Rapids: Wm. B. Eerdmans Publishing Company.

_____. *The Pulpit Commentary, John (Series 39), Vol. 1.* H. P. Reynolds, expositor. New York: Funk & Wagnalls Co. Reprinted, Grand Rapids: Wm. B. Eerdmans Publishing Company.

_____. *The Pulpit Commentary, Matthew (Series 34), Vol. 2.* W. A. Williams, expositor. New York: Funk & Wagnalls Co. Reprinted, Grand Rapids: Wm. B. Eerdmans Publishing Company.

Stokes, George Thomas. *The Expositor's Bible, Acts.* New York: A.C. Armstrong Co., 1903. Reprinted, Grand Rapids: Baker Book House.

Strassfeld, Michael and Sharon. *The Second Jewish Catalog.* Philadelphia: Jewish Publication Society of America, 1976.

Wuest, Kenneth S. *Hebrews in the Greek New Testament.* Grand Rapids: Wm. B. Eerdmans Publishing Company, 1951.

Zimmerman, Martha. *Celebrate the Feasts.* Minneapolis: Bethany Fellowship Inc., 1981.